ems should '
vn below
owers '
hone

GREAT
IRISH
HEROES

Sean McMahon

MERCIER PRESS
IRISH PUBLISHER – IRISH STORY

MERCIER PRESS

Cork

www.mercierpress.ie

Revised and abridged version of *Great Irish Heroes* published in 2008 by Mercier Press.

© Sean McMahon, 2018

ISBN: 978 1 78117 579 8

10 9 8 7 6 5 4 3 2 1

A CIP record for this title is available from the British Library.

Printed and bound in the EU.

CONTENTS

FOREWORD

The dictionary defines 'hero' variously as: a man or woman of distinguished bravery; an illustrious person; a person reverenced or idealised; the principal figure in a work of literary or dramatic art. Both real people, and mythical ones too, are covered in this generous spectrum of meaning. Here, the figures dancing in a national frieze astound us with their variety, their courage, their achievements and their Irishness. This last quality is usually achieved by being born here and having a main sphere of activity here. But some born here achieved heroic greatness, of whatever kind, far from the oul sod, and a few, though born elsewhere, made Ireland their local habitation.

The list includes saints and scholars, soldiers and statesmen, pirates and politicians, poets, mathematicians, founders and feminists, martyrs and survivors and bold Fenian men. We stride down the ages and meet a host of outstanding, and sometimes unlikely, heroes.

Ireland is full of heroes – this book could be ten times as large. This is just a heroic handful and it is fitting to remember their glories and rejoice in their heroism.

MARY AIKENHEAD

Founder of the Religious Sisters of Charity
1787–1858

MARY AIKENHEAD was born in Daunt's Square, off the Grand Parade in Cork, on 19 January 1787. She was the eldest daughter of David Aikenhead, a wealthy Protestant doctor of Scottish descent, and Mary Stackpoole, a Catholic heiress. Mary was baptised into her father's Anglican religion at St Anne's church in Shandon but was fostered, because of ill-health, by a poor Catholic family called Rorke, who lived in a small cottage on Eason's Hill, a poor country area behind Shandon. She stayed there for six years, receiving weekly visits from her parents and only being allowed home to make a brief acquaintance with her younger siblings: Anne, Margaret and St

John. Her return home at age six was made less traumatic by the incorporation into the Aiken-head household of her beloved foster parents, 'Mammy Rorke' and 'Daddy John'.

Whatever motives lay behind the fosterage, it had the effect of acquainting Mary with the dire poverty in parts of the city, and the memory of her sojourn there was to prove significant in her later vocation. It also was her introduction to Catholicism, as she went to mass with the Rorkes.

Her father also knew the poor areas of the city well, since he ministered, often unpaid, to the poor of Cork. By the time of his death in 1801, his teenage daughter realised just how necessary and unusual this practical charity was. She was strangely moved when her father converted to Catholicism on his deathbed. She had continued to attend mass regularly, but secretly, so as not to offend him. Soon she was taking instruction and was received into the Church on 6 June 1802, when she was in her sixteenth year. Her two sisters and brother followed her into the faith of their mother.

When Mary was twenty-two she went to stay with a married friend, Anna Maria O'Brien, in Dublin and, joining her in charitable work, found conditions in the poorer parts of the city indescribable. Still very religious, she resisted a strong vocation because all of the existing religious orders were enclosed and, while fully supporting that kind of calling, she felt hers was intended to be more practical.

While in Dublin, Mary met Daniel Murray, who later became archbishop of Dublin, and he chose her to be the founder member of a congregation called the Sisters of Charity. He also gave his support to Catherine McAuley, who founded another religious order, the Sisters of Mercy.

Mary thought it essential to have training in

the religious life and so, with a companion, Alicia Walsh, she endured a rigorous novitiate at the Convent of the Institute of the Blessed Virgin in York from 6 June 1812 to August 1815. The two made their vows of perpetual profession privately to Murray and, with assent from Pope Pius VII, initiated the Pious Congregation of the Religious Sisters of Charity on 9 December 1816. As well as the usual vows of poverty, chastity and obedience, there was a vow of service to the poor, with a particular emphasis on visiting people in their homes. One of their first foundations was in North William Street, off Summerhill, in north Dublin; a second was in Stanhope Street. The authorities in the grim Kilmainham Gaol invited the sisters to visit the convicts. Mary, superior-general of the order, made the women on the death wing her special concern.

Of the members of her immediate family, St John died young, Margaret married a doctor and went to live in Kerry, and Anne, in 1823, joined the order in Stanhope Street.

In 1824 Bishop of Cork John Murphy asked Dr Murray to let him have a community of Sisters of Charity in his diocese. Dr Murray referred the matter to Mary, who was delighted at the prospect of having a community in her native city. However, Dr Murphy wanted to have the Sisters under his own jurisdiction, whereas the Congregation had been established as one with a central governing body. Having consulted Dr Murray, Fr Peter Kenney, SJ, and Fr Robert St Leger, SJ, Mary informed Bishop Murphy that she could not accede to his request. Although this did not please him, Bishop Murphy decided that, even if they weren't under his jurisdiction, he still wanted the Sisters of Charity in Cork, and in September 1826 the sisters moved into the house provided for them. This proved to be a ramshackle building, which the sisters jokingly called Cork Castle. It was to be their home for nineteen years before they finally acquired St Vincent's Convent on Peacock Lane. The order had by then won much praise for their succouring of the poor, especially during the great cholera outbreak of 1832.

Realising the need for a hospital for the needy in Dublin, in 1834 Mary bought the townhouse of Lord Meath in St Stephen's Green for £3,000 (about €270,000 today) and opened it as St Vincent's, the first Catholic hospital in Ireland and the first run by nuns. Medical expertise was obtained by sending members of the order to Paris for training. By this time Mary had begun to show signs of inflammation of the spine, which severely debilitated her but did not stop her work.

In 1838, at the request of John Polding, archbishop of Sydney, the Sisters of Charity established a community in his city. Convents were also opened in Waterford in 1842, Galway in 1844 and Clonmel in 1845.

Though crippled with spinal troubles, dropsy and eventual paralysis, Mary continued to work prodigiously. In 1845 she moved to Our Lady's Mount in the rustic village of Harold's Cross, south of Dublin city. It was there that she died on 22 July 1858, having spent many years of her heroic life in a wheelchair. Her coffin was carried to the graveyard in Donnybrook by working-class men.

Mary was commemorated on an Irish postage stamp in 1958, the centenary of her death.

GEORGE BOOLE

Mathematician
1815–1864

GEORGE BOOLE was born in Lincoln on 2 November 1815, the eldest child of John, a shoemaker with an interest in mathematics and instrument-making. His mother, Mary Ann Joyce, was a lady's maid. George was not born until nine years after their marriage on 14 September 1806. Three other children, Mary Ann, William and Charles, followed quickly over the next five years.

George was a sickly baby and not expected to survive, but he defied expectations and showed early indications of unusual intellectual ability. By the time he was eight he had outpaced his father in mathematical knowledge, and deeply depressed a local bookseller who had offered to teach him Latin, by translating Virgil and Horace by the age of twelve and learning Ancient Greek by himself. This ability in the Classics caused a local storm when he translated a poem by the Greek poet Meleager; his father was so proud that he had it published. A local schoolmaster hotly denied that any lad of fourteen could produce such work. But of course that lad had been taught mathematics by his father from an early age and, fluent in French, German and Italian, was appointed a teacher in Heigham's School in Doncaster before his sixteenth birthday.

In fact, it was necessary for him to work to earn money to keep the family because his father's business had failed.

By the time he was nineteen, George found it advantageous to return to Lincoln and open up his own school. He spent what free time he had studying mathematics, finding his ability in its more obscure aspects greater even than his linguistic skills. Textbooks were expensive and hard to find but Boole was able to make use of the libraries in the local Mechanics Institute, the virtually free source of adult education that most sizable towns possessed at the time. Soon he was an expert on such standard mathematical works as Newton's *Principia* and the works of the French mathematician and astronomer Laplace and Italian mathematician and astronomer Lagrange.

In 1838, when he was twenty-three, George moved to Waddington, a village five miles south of Lincoln. There he ran a boarding school known as Hall's Academy with the help of his family, for whom the school was the only source of income. He began to publish papers on all aspects of modern calculus, gradually building up an international reputation as a modern master. In 1844 he won the Royal Society's medal for a paper 'On a General Method in Analysis', which used algebraic methods for the solution of differential equations.

This honour encouraged him to apply for the chair of mathematics in the new Queen's Colleges set up in 1845 in Ireland by Sir Robert Peel to appease the Repealers. His sponsors included Augustus de Morgan, who was fascinated by Boole's work on logic, and the future Lord Kelvin. In November 1849 he was appointed as the first Professor of Mathematics at Queen's College Cork (now University College Cork) and quickly gained a reputation for brilliance and dedication. He was elected Dean of Science in 1851, by which time he had met Mary Everest, whose uncle, George Everest, had surveyed the Indian subcontinent and had the highest Himalayan mountain named after him. Boole was seventeen years older, but, when her father died and left her penniless, he asked Mary to marry him. The marriage, which proved extremely happy, was solemnised on 11 September 1855 in her home village of Wickwar in Gloucester. They had five daughters, the youngest of whom, Ethel Lilian (1864–1960), became famous as a novelist. She was the author of *The Gadfly* (1897).

With more leisure time in Cork than he had as a teacher, Boole was now able to work on his most significant contribution to mathematical theory. In 1854 he published *An Investigation of the Laws of Thought, on which are founded the Mathematical Theories of Logic and Probabilities*. It was the first introduction to Boolean algebra and claimed logic as a mathematical discipline and not a philosophical one, as it had earlier been treated.

The Boolean system remained relatively ignored until modern electronic researchers, particularly Claude Shannon, realised that its structure fitted exactly that of circuitry. The language and mechanisms devised since then have brought about the greatest surge of invention since the discovery of the wheel. The computer used for the writing of this book is the result of a rapid evolution for which the genius son of a Lincolnshire cobbler must take much of the credit.

Boole continued to run his department and to publish mind-stretching papers. At forty-two he was elected a Fellow of the Royal Society, and he received honorary degrees from Dublin and Oxford Universities. His *Treatise on Differential Equations* (1859) and *Treatise on the Calculus of Finite Differences* (1860) were further examples of his brilliance, but sadly his work on probability, so vital for actuaries and space walkers, had not been fully developed at the time of his death.

He lived two miles from the college and one winter's day gave his lectures soaked to the skin after walking there in the pouring rain. He caught pneumonia, a dangerous disease in those years before the invention of sulfa drugs and antibiotics. Mary, who had some idea of homeopathic medicine, kept dowsing his bed with buckets of water, but he died on 8 December 1864, not long into his forty-ninth year, at the height of his career.

He is remembered in University College Cork, where the library and an underground lecture area are named in his honour.

BRIAN BORU

'Emperor of the Irish'
c. 941–1014

BRIAN MAC CENNÉTIG, aka Brian Bóruma and known in English as Brian Boru, was born *c.* 941 in the territory of his people, the Dál gCais, who held land on both sides of the Shannon, parts of the present-day counties of Clare and Limerick. His familiar name came from his birthplace Béal Bóramha, near Killaloe in Clare. He became king of Munster, ruler of the Leth Moga (the southern half of Ireland marked by a line from Dublin to Galway Bay and the traditional territory of the Eóganacht clan) and *árd rí* (high king) of the whole country, and was given the title *Imperator Scotorum* ('Emperor of the Irish') by his confessor, Máel Suthain. He gained power by ruthlessness in warfare and surprising benevolence in victory.

The Dalcassians had come to prominence when the Dál gCais chieftain, Cennétig Mac Lorcáin, Brian's father, had challenged the hegemony of the Uí Néill. Brian trained the Dalcassian army and assumed command on the death of Mathgamain, his older brother. He avenged his brother's treacherous killing by the Limerick Ostmen (as the settled Scandinavians called themselves) by killing their king, Ímar, and his sons in the church of St Senan on Scattery Island near Kilrush, thus sacrilegiously disregarding the tradition of sanctuary.

Brian also learned from the Norsemen, the most belligerent of the Scandinavians, about the use of naval tactics in battle. His great aquatic highway, the Shannon, and the rivers Slaney, Barrow, Nore, Suir and Blackwater gave him access to Leinster. The original Norse invaders

had used the rivers to pene-
trate the inland Irish settlements on their plun-
dering incursions and
Brian used their tactics
in his internal wars.

There is, however,
another Brian Boru
beyond the clever tac-
tician and diplomat.
When, at the end of
the eighteenth century, a
slowly resurgent Ireland was
able to begin to cherish its heroes,
Brian Boru became a symbol of a once great and
unconquered land. A country emerging from
psychological shock after centuries of defeat and
subjection found it salutary to take pride in such a
hero. Tom Moore, their Minstrel Boy, urged Erin
to remember the days of old and also the glories

of Brian for, 'Enough of his glory remains on each blade/To light us to victory yet.'

As the condition of the Irish improved after the horrors of the Famine, Brian came to be revered as a near-saint as well as the archetypal warrior. Most Irish parochial halls had on their wall a picture of the saintly Brian kneeling at a crucifix in his tent at Clontarf about to have his venerable and still crowned head hacked off by the evil Viking mercenary Brodar, who, fleeing from the battle, stumbled upon the king by accident. This scene was also illustrated in most primary school readers. He was the exemplary pious king who defeated the wicked Danes and saved the island for Christianity. It was also noted that he died on Good Friday.

To be truthful, the hagiography began early, after the publication of the twelfth-century *Cogadh Gaedhel re Gallaibh* ('The War of the Gaedhil with the Gaill'), a pseudo-historical account of the activities of the Viking marauders in the ninth and tenth centuries, and of the resistance of Brian and Mathgamain, culminating in the final defeat at Clontarf on 23 April 1014. It was almost certainly commissioned by Muirchertach Ua Briain (d. 1119), Brian's great-grandson, for use as propaganda in his bid for the high-kingship against the Uí Néill.

One of the distortions passed down to modern times, apart from the saintliness of Brian, was the belief that his last enemies were the Danes. In fact, of all the Scandinavians the Danes were the least warlike, the ones most interested in settling down to a life of commerce. The decisive battle of Clontarf was, in fact, between two armies made up of Ostmen and Irish. The Leinster Ostmen were led by Sitric, who was Brian's son-in-law, and Máel Mórda Mac Murchada, the king of Leinster, whose sister Gormflaith had been married to both Brian and his supporting general, Máel Sechnaill. (He was the Malachy who 'wore the collar of gold that he won from the proud invader'.) The Leinster side also had allies from Viking settlements in Man, the Hebrides, the Orkneys and Iceland under the general command of Sigurd, who, the contemporary equivalent of the tabloid press claimed, had come because the bewitching Gormflaith had offered herself as an extra inducement.

The battle, which undoubtedly crushed the militancy if not the commercial acuity of the Ostmen, was important enough to figure in the thirteenth-century *Story of Burnt Njal*, the most famous of the heroic sagas of Iceland. It includes a slightly fictionalised form of the story of Clontarf and Brian's death, and refers to the remarkable Gormflaith as Kormlada. The Munstermen (with their Ostmen allies from Limerick, now reconciled to the *árd rí*) won the battle but the cost was high. Murchad, Brian's son and best captain, and Murchad's son Turloch both died, robbing the short-lived dynasty of its heirs. Brian's other sons were weak and indecisive, so the hope of a strong and united Ireland waned, and the *Imperium Scotorum* passed like an unlikely dream.

Under Brian there had been a decade of peace and artistic, ecclesiastic and academic development. He made good the destruction of the Norsemen, rebuilding monasteries and libraries, and establishing the primacy of Armagh, the place where he tacitly accepted the imperial title. The older chroniclers made much of his triumphal circuit round the quasi-united country, 'keeping the sea on his left hand'. It used to be thought that a sobriquet given to Brian – 'of the tributes' – referred to the adulation, real and organised, that greeted him on this royal progress, but it may have been referencing something as simple as refusing to pay the yearly tribute of cattle to the Eóganacht, the previous rulers of Munster.

Brian's private life was characteristic of the aristocracy of the time, affected by the need to make political alliances. He married four women: Mór, the mother of his favourite son Murchad; Echrad; the stellar Gormflaith; and Dub Choblaig, daughter of the king of Connacht.

After he was killed on Good Friday, 23 April 1014, his body was taken to Armagh for burial in what is now the grounds of the Church of Ireland cathedral there. Even then, there was some kind of a sense of sanctity about this authentic Irish hero.

BRENDAN
THE NAVIGATOR

Monastic Founder and Voyager
c. 484–*c.* 578

BRENDAN was born *c.* 484 at Ciarraighe Luachra near Tralee in County Kerry. He was baptised by Erc of Ardfert in the same county and placed under the care of Ita, known as the 'Brigid of Munster', in her convent at Killeedy. When he was six he was put into the care of Erc, who tutored him until he was ready to attend the great teaching monasteries of Jarlath of Tuam, Finnian of Clonard and Enda of Aran, with the proviso from Erc: 'Come back to me that you may receive priestly orders from my hand before I die.'

Erc ordained him in 512 and over the next

eighteen years Brendan founded a number of monasteries, although the one most closely associated with his name, at Clonfert, County Galway, not far from the Shannon, was founded in 558–64, in the latter part of his life. It joined the foundations of Jarlath, Finnian and Enda as a great monastic school. Another foundation, at Annaghdown on the shores of Lough Corrib, he gave into the control of his sister, Briga, as a convent for nuns. One small cell associated with him was Shanakeel (Sean-Chill, 'old church'), sited at the foot of Mount Brandon, near Tralee. He founded yet another monastery on Arran in the Inner Hebrides and eventually made his way as far north as the Faroe islands and Iceland. He worked in Scotland establishing monastic houses in Tiree and Perthshire, and it is believed that he met his fellow Irish missionary, Colum Cille, on the island of Hinba in the Outer Hebrides. He is also believed to have travelled to Brittany with the

Welshman Malo (who left his name there) and to have stayed in Wales with Cadoc, founder of the abbey of Llancarfan.

It was probably because of these successful travels that his name was associated with the *Navigatio Sancti Brendani* ('Voyage of St Brendan'), dating from the ninth or tenth century. In it the saint, with sixty companions, travelled far west of Iceland, reaching America (the Vikings called it Vinland) long before either Leif Erikson around AD 1,000, or Christopher Columbus at the end of the fifteenth century. It is said that Columbus had with him a manuscript entitled *Navigatio Sancti Brendani Abbatis* on his journey to the New World.

The *Navigatio* takes the form of a recognised literary form, called an *immram* in Old Irish, that describes the wonders seen and experienced by voyagers. Typical of this form is the *Immram Curaig Maíle Dúin* ('Voyage of Máel

Dúin's Currach'), the ninth-century tale used by Tennyson for one of his narrative poems. The voyagers usually come ashore in a kind of ideal land, not unlike Tír na nÓg ('the land of youth'), the Irish equivalent of Valhalla.

In an age in which miracles were thought possible, wonders were associated with charismatic characters like the saint. One story describes how he constructed a cell on top of Mount Brandon (also named for him) which, on a clear day, gave views for 100 miles. From there, it is said, he had a vision of a promised land. The myth of a lost land like Atlantis lying somewhere to the west of Ireland was a common one; as Gerald Griffin's poem puts it: 'they called it Hy-Brasil, the isle of the Blest'.

The voyaging saint was a convenient hook on which to hang the mixture of fact, fantasy and plagiarism that constitutes the *Navigatio*. Its author is thought to have been an Irish *peregrinus* ('missionary exile'), one of many like Colum Cille and Columbanus who imposed upon themselves the 'white martyrdom' of permanent exile from their beloved homeland to preach the gospel of Christ in pagan Europe. At least 120 manuscripts are still in existence, some in Latin, others in early German and French, and the purpose was as much devotional as entertainment.

In the story told in the *Navigatio*, the saint and his companions, having fasted for forty days before embarking, converse with St Patrick and also come across Judas Iscariot clinging to an ocean rock on day-release from Hell. They land on a large island at Eastertide, but when the Paschal ceremonies are completed the 'island' begins to move. The terrified voyagers run back to their boat. Many believe the island, luxuriant with fruit and flowers, is a description of the state of Florida. The belief that such a voyage was actually possible was reinforced when Tim

Severin and his companions reached St John's, Newfoundland, at 8 p.m. on 26 June 1977 in a replica of a sixth-century craft.

Brendan, his travelling done, made his way to his sister's community in Annaghdown, where he died around AD 577/578. His finest memorial, the magnificent Irish-Romanesque cathedral at Clonfert, was built in the twelfth century by Conor Maenmoy O'Kelly, and gave its name to the diocese east of Galway.

In April 1994 Postverk Føroya, the philatelic office of the Faroe Islands, issued two stamps designed by Colin Harrison commemorating the saint's landing in the Faroes and Iceland.

TURLOUGH CAROLAN

Blind Harpist
1670–1738

TOIRDHEALBHACH Ó CEARBHALLÁIN, as he would have spelled his name while he lived, was born in the townland of Spiddal near Nobber, County Meath in 1670. His father was an iron founder and he moved with his family to Ballyfarnan, County Roscommon, in the year 1684, where there was work to be had at the iron foundry belonging to the MacDermott Roe family at Alderford near the village. Turlough was a clever lad and Mrs MacDermott Roe seemed to realise his potential. She had him educated with her own children and encouraged his writing of verse in both English and Irish. When he was eighteen he was blinded by the endemic smallpox and his practical patron had him taught music as one of the few means of livelihood open to the blind. She arranged for him to have tuition over three years, supporting him until he was able to fly free at twenty-one. She supplied him with a horse and a guide, and for the next fifty years he lived the not-unhappy life of an itinerant musician. During his career, he had a reputation for cheerfulness and gregariousness, and seldom referred to his affliction.

The late seventeenth and eighteenth centuries saw the fullest richness of baroque music and it is interesting that Turlough's work shows affinities with that of the more famous Italians: Corelli, Geminiani and especially Vivaldi, his slightly younger contemporary. Turlough's musicological reputation rests mainly on his compositions rather than virtuoso playing.

In Ireland it was the time of the Protestant Ascendancy's domination, especially after the

Treaty of Limerick (1691). The Irish aristocracy, who previously would have been the patrons of the arts and a natural resource for those such as Turlough, had mostly disappeared, to be replaced by an alien nobility. The native Irish, largely deprived of leaders, became an under-class and, until the relief acts at the end of the eighteenth century, could do little but accept their lot. It was lucky for Turlough that not all the Ascendancy landlords were absentees and some had sufficient taste to welcome native artists.

His first patron was George Reynolds, from the neighbouring county of Leitrim, who seems to have been the first to recommend that Turlough compose his own tunes. One early piece that he named *Sí Bheag, Sí Mhór* (little fairy mound, big fairy mound) was based upon an old tale from his native Meath about two giants who were turned into fairy mounds by a wizard.

Turlough made a habit of attaching the

name of a host to a piece specially written for a visit. Once, on a journey home from Tulsk in Roscommon to his house in Mohill, County Leitrim, he called at the house of a friend, Dr John Stafford, who invited him to dinner. The food was good, the whiskey was better, and Turlough 'forgot' to go home. Next morning he composed the tune 'Carolan's Receipt for Dr John Stafford'. (The word 'receipt' then was used as the equivalent of a thank-you letter.) Other tunes were named 'Dr John Hart, Bishop of Achonry'; 'Eleanor Plunkett'; 'Fanny Power'; 'George Brabazon'; 'John O'Connor'; 'Lord Inchiquin'; 'Planxty Irwin'; 'Planxty Burke' and 'Planxty Browne'. (The word 'planxty' is defined as 'a harp tune of sportive or animated character, moving in triplets'. It is not an Irish word and according to the dictionary may have been invented by Carolan himself. It can be danced to, but the tempo is slower than that of a jig.)

The preservation of many of his tunes was due to the excellent work of the assiduous collector Edward Bunting, who was official note-taker at the Belfast Harp Festival of 1792. Leading Irish groups such as Planxty, the Chieftains and the Dubliners have played Turlough's music to their advantage. Thanks to an excellent recording by Seán Ó Riada, 'Carolan's Concerto' became an entry in the charts. Even before this, the tune, arranged as a martial slow march, was played by the Foot Guards at the annual Trooping of the Colour in Horse Guards Parade in Whitehall, to celebrate the British monarch's birthday.

Turlough's rovings were mainly in Connacht and Ulster, and though, for obvious reasons, he preferred the houses of the rich for shelter, he entertained the lowly with equal pleasure. He married Mary Maguire from Fermanagh and had a house built for her in Mohill. Their marriage seems to have been happy, though he knew many other women. They had seven children, and when she died in 1733, he wrote an elegy in her honour, containing the couplet:

Fágadh 'na ndéidh sin liom féin go brónach
I ndeireadh mo shaoil's gan mo chéile bheith beo agam.
(Bereft after that alone and in despair
At the end of my time, with no wife to ease care.)

Turlough did not confine his compositions or his performances to the houses of the great. He played at wakes and weddings, and at every country ball, and, in each case, if he was late the ceremonies were postponed. He was, of course, fond of liquor; in the culture of the time he could hardly avoid it. There is a story that his final composition was dedicated to the butler who brought him his last drink.

This drink would have been drunk in the home of the MacDermott Roes in Roscommon, to which he returned when he felt the hand of death upon him. He had taken ill in the village of Tempo in County Fermanagh but made his way to Alderford. It was essentially a homecoming, for he owed much to that family. He died on 25 March 1738 and his wake, attended by eleven brother harpists, lasted for four days. He is buried in the churchyard of Ballyfarnan and in nearby Keadue the O'Carolan Harp Festival and Summer School is held every year. There is a sufficient case to consider him as Ireland's premier composer and he figured on the last £50 banknote before the introduction of the Euro.

EDWARD CARSON

Lawyer and Political Leader
1854–1935

EDWARD HENRY CARSON was born at 4 Harcourt Street, Dublin on 9 February 1854, the son of an architect. He was educated at Portarlington, Wesley College and Trinity College, Dublin, where he took his BA and MA and was a prominent member of the university's hurling team. Completing his legal training at King's Inns, he was called to the Irish Bar in 1877 and made a QC in London in 1889. He built up a wide legal practice and was called to prosecute many cases arising out of the Land League agitation, earning him the sobriquet 'Coercion Carson'. It was, however, as a defence counsel that he became famous and infamous in the courts.

His granitic, chiselled face, used to great effect in the English courts, more than compensated for the Dublin accent that he never lost.

In 1906 Carson took on the Admiralty over the unjust dismissal of a cadet, George Archer-Shee, from the Osborne Naval Cadet College on the Isle of Wight. The case became so famous that Sir Terence Rattigan wrote a successful play called *The Winslow Boy* (1946) based on the story.

However, an earlier case was arguably much more dramatic: he was the defence counsel for the Marquess of Queensberry in the libel suit brought against him by Oscar Wilde, a fellow Trinity undergraduate. On hearing that Carson was to defend Queensberry, Wilde could not resist the typically paradoxical remark: 'I am sure that he will do so with all the added bitterness of an old friend.' Epigrams do not always have to be literally true; Carson and he were merely acquaintances, Wilde regarding him as a worthy plodder who had won none of the glittering prizes that seemed to fall into his own lap. He was sure he would be able to withstand wittily any cross-examination that his fellow Dubliner could muster, using the accent that he had long discarded. In fact, Carson slaughtered Wilde with a searing Irish wit of his own, and the jury, alienated by Wilde's elegant, camp arrogance, found Queensberry not guilty. Two hours later Wilde was arrested for sodomy. Carson, to his credit, tried to have that case dropped.

Carson's earnings were enormous, allowing him to maintain two houses: one in London and the other at Rottingdean in Sussex, where he lived with his sickly wife, Annette Kirwan from Galway, and their four children, William (1880), Aileen (1881), Gladys (1885) and Walter (1890).

His career in politics began on 20 June 1892 when he was appointed solicitor-general for Ireland. Later that year he was elected Unionist

MP for the University of Dublin. In 1893 he was admitted to the English Bar by the Honourable Society of the Middle Temple and from then on practised mainly in London. Almost as a matter of course, seven years later, on 7 May 1900, he was appointed solicitor-general for England and received an *ex officio* knighthood.

Carson was aware that should the main British parties fail to maintain a majority in government, the Irish Parliamentary Party under John Redmond might one day hold the balance of power and would demand the dreaded Home Rule for Ireland as the price of their acquiescence. This is exactly what happened in 1910, when the general election of that year reduced the Liberal majority. The results of a second general election held in December 1910 still left the Irish Party holding the balance. The 1911 Parliamentary Act removed the House of Lords' ability to block a Commons bill, so Carson, now head of the Irish

Unionist Party, warned the unionists of Ulster that they must prepare to resist Home Rule by all means.

Carson found an ideal partner for his campaign to preserve the union in the leader of the Ulster Unionist Party, James Craig, who had military experience in the Boer War and was a brilliant organiser. Both men encouraged the militarism of the Ulster Volunteer Force (UVF), which had used the unionist Orange Order as its nucleus. Carson was the first to sign the Solemn League and Covenant in September 1912, a statement of intent to oppose Home Rule by any means necessary, and he gave his full approval to illegal gun-running and the setting-up of a provisional government for Ulster. When the Home Rule Bill (offering the mere minimum of self-government) was passed on 25 May 1914 and seemed certain of receiving the royal assent, it looked like a civil war was imminent. Only the

Craig and Carson

much bloodier Great War caused its postponement until the war should be over.

In 1916 the Easter Rising made a 'temporary' partition of the country inevitable and in December 1920 the Government of Ireland Act provided for separate governments in Belfast and Dublin. Carson hated this 'solution' to the 'Irish Question', and was particularly incensed at the terms of the 1921 Treaty which created the Irish Free State. Yet he also had little sympathy for Orangeism, once stating that their speeches reminded him of 'the unrolling of a mummy; all bones and rotten rags'.

Carson did not live in Ireland in the 1920s, preferring the life of one of seven Lords of Appeal and membership of the House of Lords as Baron Carson of Duncairn. He was subject to debilitating hypochondria all his adult life and, before Germany had become the enemy, made regular visits to the spa at Bad Homburg. Lady Annette had died on 6 April 1913 at the height of the UVF agitation, and on 17 September 1914 he married Ruby Frewen, a Yorkshire woman thirty-one years his junior, by whom he had one son, Edward. In 1933 he was present when the statue by L. S. Merrifield that dominates the long drive up to the parliamentary buildings at Stormont was unveiled. He died at his home in Kent on 22 October 1935 and was given a state funeral and buried in St Anne's cathedral in Belfast.

MICHAEL COLLINS

Revolutionary and Statesman
1890–1922

MICHAEL COLLINS was born on 16 October 1890 at Woodfield, Clonakilty, in West Cork, the son of a small farmer. The youngest of eight children, six of whom emigrated, he attended Clonakilty National School and at fifteen passed the British civil service entry examination. He moved to London, where he lived with his sister Hannie and took up a position in the Post Office Savings Bank in Kensington. He later worked in several finance houses, including the London office of the Guaranty Trust Company of New York, an experience that helped him in his role as finance minister in the first Dáil Éireann in 1919. In this role he was able to raise a loan of

£380,000 (about €12 million today) in redeemable bonds to be repaid by an independent Ireland.

In the early twentieth century London was full of Irish people, including the poet Francis A. Fahy, who was the first president of the London branch of the Gaelic League, the writer Pádraig Ó Conaire, and the Belfast-born Presbyterian nationalist Robert Lynd. Collins joined the Gaelic League and the GAA in London, and in 1909 he also joined the Irish Republican Brotherhood (IRB). On becoming aware of the planned Easter Rising in 1916, he went to Dublin to take part, acting as Joseph Plunkett's aide-de-camp in the General Post Office.

In the aftermath of Patrick Pearse's surrender, like many of the men arrested in General Sir John Maxwell's general sweep, Collins was imprisoned in Frongoch, in present-day Gwynedd. Even in prison, he was notable for his swagger, his viciousness during friendly bouts of wrestling and his organisational ability. It was his aura of confidence that earned him the sobriquet 'The Big Fellow'.

In Frongoch, Collins helped reorganise the IRB, which vocally advocated armed resistance as 'the indispensable factor in our struggle for freedom'. Released in December 1916, he returned to Ireland and began to reorganise the entire republican movement. He was part of the team that successfully sprang Éamon de Valera from Lincoln Jail in 1918.

The Great War ended on 11 November 1918 and in the general election that followed in December, Sinn Féin won 73 of the 105 Irish seats. Their refusal to sit at Westminster and their rejection of the original terms promised under the 1912 Home Rule Bill were indications of a bloody war to come.

Officially starting in January 1919, the War of Independence was a guerrilla war and often consisted of attacks on the Royal Irish Constabulary

(RIC) by the IRA, the army of the newly set up Irish parliament, Dáil Éireann. From March 1920, when the IRA carried out a raid or a killing, the response of the newly recruited reserve of the RIC known as the 'Black and Tans' (after a famous pack of Limerick hunting hounds) was often disproportionate. The addition to the RIC in July 1920 of the Auxiliary Division, who were, if anything, even more violent and given to looting than the Tans, deepened the misery that the country had to suffer and increased the resolve of the IRA. Britain's stock internationally was never lower, but Prime Minister David Lloyd George and Secretary of State Winston Churchill seemed unconcerned.

Collins proved an effective leader during the war. He built up an intelligence network that had invaluable 'spies in the Castle', David Neligan and Ned Broy, and he developed the 'Squad', his killing team. The Squad eliminated, among others, District Inspector Oswald Swanzy, believed to have ordered the assassination of Tomás MacCurtáin, the Sinn Féin lord mayor of Cork, in March 1920, and Lee Wilson, the officer who in 1916 had paraded the ageing Tom Clarke naked in view of the nurses in the Rotunda Hospital, outside which the Irish prisoners were being held.

Incidents such as the attempted elimination of the 'Cairo Gang' by the Squad in November 1920 caused a price of £10,000 (about €320,000 today) to be put on Collins' head. The 'Gang' was a group of British soldiers who had been brought to Ireland to conduct intelligence operations against the IRA. One member, Major George Smyth, came to Ireland to avenge the shooting of his brother, Lieutenant Colonel Brice Smyth, on 17 July 1920. Smyth, a one-armed, much-decorated British Army veteran, had obtained notoriety when he addressed a company of RIC officers in Listowel with the words: 'The more you shoot the better we will like you …'

The actions of the Squad on what would later become known as 'Bloody Sunday', provoked a savage response. The killing of fourteen men that morning, only some of whom were members of the 'Cairo Gang', were followed, on the same day, by the notorious attack on a GAA game in Croke Park, when British forces turned their guns on the crowd, killing twelve people.

Collins was a brilliant organiser and enjoyed eluding the authorities in feats of daring that made him a kind of Green Pimpernel. He used his limited spare time to consider what might be the most appropriate form of government when Ireland would have her freedom. He also worried about the plight of nationalists in the north where, especially in the east, Catholics were regularly at the mercy of the UVF, now legitimised as the Ulster Special Constabulary.

The Truce of July 1921 came as a relief to all, especially the British. Collins soon found himself, along with Arthur Griffith, the founder of Sinn Féin, on the delegation that was to hammer out the terms of the Anglo-Irish Treaty in London. Before Collins left London, he wrote in a letter that when he signed the Treaty he had 'signed his death warrant'.

The agreement gave what Collins saw as 'the best foothold for final progress', but a minority in the Dáil cabinet and in Dáil Éireann rejected it. De Valera, who had deliberately refused to be a delegate, resigned from his position as president of the Irish Republic. The stage was set for a civil war as brother turned against brother. Following an election in May 1922, which gave the pro-Treaty candidates an overwhelming majority, Collins assumed command of the new Free State army, while William T. Cosgrave became chairman of the government. Civil war broke out on 28 June.

In August Collins left Dublin for a tour of Munster, where the bitterest fighting was taking place. On 22 August his convoy was ambushed at Béal na mBláth in West Cork, twelve miles from his birthplace, and a bullet wound in the head proved fatal. The reaction of his soldiers, apart from bitter grief, was savagery against any IRA members they could find.

Ireland's most charismatic leader had died at the wrong hands and the wrong time for the Free State and the northern nationalists. The country was already bereft with the death of Griffith on 12 August and this further blow was almost more than it could bear.

COLUM CILLE

Saint and Exile
521–597

COLUM CILLE is the premier Ulster saint, second only in reputation to St Patrick, with whom tradition claims he shares a grave. The belief is old: the Norman overlord John de Courcy (d. 1219) wrote a Latin verse about it:

In burgo Duno tumulo
Tumulantur in uno
Brigida, Patricius
Atque Columba Pius.

(In Down three saints one grave do fill
Brigid, Patrick and Colum Cille.)

In this and in nearly every other aspect of his life,

it is virtually impossible to peel away the accumulation of stories with which nearly 1,500 years of piety have layered him. It is not hard to see why: he was a giant figure in the Church of the time and the monasteries with which his name is associated – Durrow, Kells and Iona – played a significant part in the development of the Irish and British Churches.

Part of the reason for his supremacy was his aristocratic connections with the long-lasting Cenél Conaill dynasty. This association may also have involved him, unwillingly, in politics and could have been one of several motives for his 'white martyrdom', as homesick Irish missionaries called their self-imposed exile.

Twelfth-century politics, too, have tended to blur the facts of his life. *Doire Calgach* (Calgach's oak-grove), as the city of Derry was originally known, was changed at that time to *Doire Coluim Cille* (the oak-grove of the saint). His name was used to confer a dignity and persuasive strength to a territory over which the Cenél Conaill and the Cenél nEógain, their dynastic rivals, were in contention. A little rewriting of history was necessary, agreed by the local high king and the leading local ecclesiastic with the best of spiritual intentions.

The sixth-century saint, however, cannot be held responsible for twelfth-century politics; his own life, as far as it can be accurately told, was fraught enough, although much of what follows is no more than reasonable speculation.

Colum Cille was born near Gartan in a part of central Donegal in Tír Chonaill ('the territory of Conaill'). His birth date is given as 7 December 521, and he was the son of King Feidlimid and Eithne, a princess from Leinster. According to the *Betha Coluim Chille* (1532), compiled by the then lord of Tír Chonaill Maghnas Ó Domhnaill (d. 1563), he was given the name Crimthann, which meant 'foxy' or 'devious'.

The *Betha* is a treasure house of all the lovingly collected folklore associated with Colum Cille and records what had been believed for centuries about the wonder saint. He was fostered with Cruithnechan, a Christian Pict, and eventually named, as he is known in Ireland today, Colum Cille (Dove of the Church), the bird usually depicted with him in iconography. In other places, especially in Scotland, he is known as Columba, the Latin word for 'dove'.

According to Adomnán, his biographer and kinsman, Colum Cille left Ireland as a 'pilgrim for Christ' in 563 to bring Christianity to Pictish Scotland, using the monastery he founded on the island of Iona, near Mull in the Inner Hebrides, as his base. The previous seventeen years had been spent in study, preaching and creating the illuminated manuscripts which still amaze us. (The *Cathach*, a Latin manuscript of the Psalms and the oldest surviving text in Ireland, is believed to be in his handwriting.) Adomnán's work, *Vita Columbae*, notes that the date of Colum Cille's departure was two years after the battle of Cúl Dreimne.

The greatest myths associated with the saint concern this battle, which took place at the foot of Ben Bulben, then the border between Ulster and Connacht. Colum Cille may indeed have been involved in this battle between Christian and pagan. The lore is that he had an enmity with Diarmait Mac Cerbaill, the *árd rí*, because of the high king's judgement – 'to every cow its calf' – in settlement of what is jocularly called the first copyright case. Finnian of Movilla (present-day Newtownards) claimed that the copy of his psalter, created so laboriously in secret and without his permission over many months by Colum Cille, should revert to him. As a result of Diarmait's judgement in Finnian's favour, Colum Cille is said to have provoked a rebellion against him, which culminated in this battle. The story continues that 3,000 people died in the battle and that the saint's confessor sent him to Pictland to win as many souls for Christ as were lost.

Whatever the reason, Colum Cille was determined to go. He took with him twelve companions, a deliberate apostolic gesture, sailing probably from Derry, and together they founded monasteries on Iona, Hinba, Tiree and Skye. Eventually, they and their successors in Iona converted not only Scotland but also much of the large British kingdom of Northumbria.

It is believed that Colum Cille returned only once to Ireland, as adviser to the great council of Druim Ceatt held near Limavady in County Derry in 575. The council was convened to settle dynastic disputes in the Dál Riata kingdom that straddled the North Channel, but the saint is said to have used the occasion to defend the *Filid*, the poet-class who had been threatened with expulsion. He won his case and was honoured by the poets as one of their own.

The saint died on Pentecost Sunday, 9 June 597. Though he appears irascible in many of the stories told about him, perhaps a reflection of a stern monastic rule, he was known in early Scots lore as Chalum-Chille Chaomh ('Colum Cille the gentle'). Soon after his death a poem, 'Amra Choluim Chille' ('Praise of Colum Cille'), attributed to Dallán Forgaill, 'the chief of the poets of Ireland', complained that like 'a harp without its strings, it is a church without its abbot'.

JAMES CONNOLLY

Revolutionary Socialist
1868–1916

JAMES CONNOLLY was born in the Cowgate, an Edinburgh slum, on 5 June 1868 to Irish immigrant parents. His father was a street cleaner and the self-educated lad was so poor that he developed rickets, a sure sign of malnutrition. He used to try to read by the light of the dying fire and used charred sticks for want of a pencil. He worked for a baker from the age of eleven, rising before sunrise in summer, and when he was fourteen joined the Second Battalion of the Royal Scots, signing on for seven years having lied about his age. He was subject to two, perhaps conflicting, ideologies as a youth: nationalism from a Fenian uncle, and socialism, engendered by the conditions he saw around him and the influence of the left-wing Scots activist John Leslie. Later he found himself able to reconcile the two elements, but leaned more and more towards nationalism in the last decade of his life.

Ironically, the army gave him his first glimpse of what he regarded as his true homeland, when he served in Cork, the Curragh and Dublin. Four months before his seven-year service was due to finish, he went AWOL from the army. He fled to Perth in Scotland, where he and Lillie Reynolds, a Protestant domestic servant from Wicklow, were married on 20 April 1889. The army records were in such a state of disarray that his superiors believed he had been discharged.

Connolly worked as a carter in Edinburgh, in conditions not much better than that of his parents, and his accent was a mixture of Irish and Scottish that would have puzzled even Professor Higgins. His spare time was spent on socialist and trade union business. In 1896 he returned to Ireland to organise the Dublin Socialist Club – later the Irish Socialist Republican Party (ISRP), said by its detractors to have more syllables than members. In 1898 he founded and edited the *Workers' Republic*, the ISRP newspaper. With its strongly Marxist content, it made slow progress, though Connolly's reputation, aided by the pungency of his essays and editorials, was becoming international.

In 1902 he went on lecture tours in Britain and America and, disappointed by the lack of progress in Britain, in 1903 went to America to work for the socialist cause. He left on 18 September and stayed for seven years. The family followed in 1904. On the day they were due to depart,

Mona, his eldest child, was burned to death when her clothes caught fire while she was preparing a meal. She was thirteen. Connolly, unaware of the cause of the family's non-arrival, anxiously haunted the landing stage at Ellis Island for a week until he was informed of the tragic news.

While in America Connolly founded the Irish Socialist Federation and produced a monthly magazine about their affairs called *The Harp*. With the Irish-born Mother Jones (Mary Harris Jones), he helped found the militant International Workers of the World (IWW), known popularly as the 'Wobblies'. It was the transatlantic equivalent of the Irish Transport and General Workers' Union (ITGWU). The ITGWU was founded by James Larkin in 1909 and Connolly was asked to come home to organise the Ulster branch. He returned to Ireland in 1910 and his stay in Belfast resulted in a successful strike for better conditions, which won more money for seamen and firemen. The efficient organisation of the Belfast dockers was remarkable, considering the sectarian climate of the northern city. Connolly was bitterly disappointed when the workers in Britain and Germany failed to revolt rather than fight in the Great War.

Connolly took over the leadership of the ITGWU when Larkin was jailed because of the 1913 strike and lockout in Dublin, and he organised the Irish Citizen Army (ICA) to protect the families of the locked-out workers. The cruelty and injustice of the lockout attracted many volunteers, including Constance Markievicz, Madeleine Ffrench-Mullen and Kathleen Lynn, who were especially pleased by the culture of gender equality in the ICA.

The existence of the ICA and its military possibilities came to the attention of Patrick Pearse and other members of the Irish Volunteers and, though there were obvious class and ideological differences, they found a common goal in possible revolution.

Connolly was made commander of the Dublin Brigade during the 1916 Rising. He had one tactical recommendation for this position – he was the only member of the war council who had any military experience. Although he was aware that the General Post Office (GPO) was undefendable, he did not anticipate its destruction. Believing that the great capitalist buildings were safe from the Empire's wrath, he was taken aback when British artillery began to reduce Sackville (now O'Connell) Street to rubble. When it became clear that the end was near, Roddy, Connolly's fifteen-year-old son, who had been acting as his (and Pearse's) aide-de-camp in the GPO, was sent home with a file of papers necessary to continue the struggle. When the Rising ended, Connolly had to countersign Pearse's surrender note because the ICA would not accept any authority but his.

Connolly knew that, as one of the signatories of the Proclamation of Independence, he would not survive. He was badly wounded and had to be carried to prison and to his court martial on a stretcher. He was strapped to a chair for his execution on 12 May because he could not stand. His was the last execution of the 1916 leaders in Ireland. After that, British Prime Minister Herbert Asquith regained control over the politically inept General Sir John Maxwell, the military governor in Ireland, who thought that his violent response would mean that 'no treason would be whispered for a hundred years'.

Connolly is remembered in street names and stations, although his socialist ideals were given little attention by the new state he helped bring about. Roddy's attempt to found an Irish Communist Party met with little success, but his father's name will forever be associated with the 'glorious thing' that was the Easter Rising of 1916.

MARGARET COUSINS

Feminist
1878–1954

MARGARET GILLESPIE was born on 7 November 1878 at the Crescent, Boyle, County Roscommon to a prosperous Methodist family. Known as Gretta, she attended the local national school and then went to the Victoria High School in Derry on a scholarship. Later a student at the Royal Irish Academy of Music, she finally graduated with a BMus from the Royal University. She taught for some years in a kindergarten and then, having met James Henry Sproull Cousins (1873–1956), a self-educated Belfast intellectual who was one of the minor figures of the Irish Literary Renaissance, married him in the Methodist church, Sandymount, in

1903. In 1902 two of James' plays, *The Sleep of the King* and *The Racing Lug*, were produced by the Irish National Dramatic Company (later the Abbey Theatre Company) in the Antient Concert Rooms in Brunswick Street, the first on 29 October and the second two nights later. The author's name was given as Séamus Ó Cúisín.

An early champion of women's rights, Gretta became an active suffragist, strongly supported by her husband. She was one of the founders, with Hanna Sheehy Skeffington, of the militant Irish Women's Franchise League in 1908. She became its treasurer and organised the Irish lecture tour of Christabel Pankhurst, the leader of the suffragette movement. She was also in the chair when Christabel's sister, Sylvia Pankhurst, addressed a 'Votes for Women' rally in Derry.

In 1910 Gretta was chosen as one of six Irish delegates to the 'Parliament of Women' in London. During her time in London she was arrested for throwing stones at 10 Downing Street, and was jailed for a month in Holloway Prison. In 1913, determined on some further direct action, she broke windows in Dublin Castle and was jailed for a month in Tullamore. She found imprisonment intolerable, calling it a 'living death'.

Gretta had become interested in Theosophy, the religious movement begun by Madame H. P. Blavatsky and Annie Besant in India, when her husband James adopted the belief in 1908, influenced by W. B. Yeats. Partly because of this, the pair, already disenchanted by the seeming lack of awareness of the rights of women and their need for a parliamentary voice in Ireland, even among nationalists, emigrated to India in 1915.

By 1916 she was the only non-Indian member of the Indian Women's University at Poonah, and she played a part in the founding of the Women's Indian Association in 1917. Though poorly supported when founded, it recently celebrated its centenary and has more than forty branches and affiliations. The association persuaded some of the members of the Madras legislature to adopt women's suffrage as a campaign.

James became literary editor of *New India*, published by Annie Besant, but his chief occupation was as principal of the Theosophical College in Madanapalle, a post he held for twenty-two years. Gretta involved herself in social and educational work, founding the National Girls School at Mangalore and acting as its first headmistress from 1919 to 1920. She became the first woman magistrate ever appointed in the Indian subcontinent and in 1928 was awarded the Founder's Silver Medal of the Theosophical Society for services to the movement.

Her days of civil disobedience were not over, however. In 1932, even though part of the legal establishment, she addressed an illegal meeting in Madras to object to special powers being incorporated in the penal code, and was imprisoned for almost a year in Vellore Women's Jail, during which she went on hunger strike to protest at the treatment of Mahatma Gandhi, who was also imprisoned. Incarceration never harmed an Irish person's reputation; after the country's independence in 1947, she was recognised as a prime contributor to India's freedom.

In 1943 she was left paralysed by a stroke, and the strength of her India-wide reputation may be measured by the monetary tributes given to ease her condition. In 1944 friends and admirers presented her with 7,000 rupees in recognition of her services to Indian women. This was supplemented by R5,000 from the government of Madras. Chakravarti Rajagopalachari, the chief minister, regularly visited her in her home. Jawaharlal Nehru, the first prime minister of the independent country, sent her a cheque for R3,000 in 1953.

Gretta published many books and articles about feminism, education, art and the history of her adopted country, finding a use for her musicological expertise in *The Music of the Orient and Occident*. She and her husband also published a joint autobiography in 1950, called *We Two Together*, that told the story of two extraordinary lives and of a remarkable contribution to women's freedom and India. She predeceased her husband by two years, dying on 11 March 1954 in Adyar in Madras, where she is buried. In 1994 President Mary Robinson unveiled a plaque to her memory in her native town of Boyle.

CÚ CHULAINN

Legendary Warrior

CÚ CHULAINN, the greatest hero of Celtic mythology, is the chief warrior of the Ulster cycle of epic tales. He is considered the Irish equivalent of Achilles. The tales represent a claim to a heroic past that was meant to serve as a model of strength, courage and nobility to later ages, and they provide stories about the prehistoric societies in which they were set. The sagas were transmitted orally and, as centuries passed, were modified, added to and often used for political purposes.

It is difficult to establish a clear biography for the Ulster warrior, but the most generally accepted sequence is that his mother is Dechtíre, the daughter of the druid Cathbad. She is spirited away to the Otherworld on the eve of her wedding to Sualtaim Mac Roth, from where she returns with a baby called Sétanta, whose immortal father is Lugh Lámhfada, the sun god. As a child Sétanta's feats of athleticism are prodigious: he is able to run fast enough to catch a ball that he himself had hit with his hurley.

He is given his famous name when as a child he is invited by Conchobar Mac Nessa to a feast at the smith Culann's house. Conchobar forgets to tell Culann that he has invited the boy and the watch dog is released to guard the house. After Sétanta kills the dog in self-defence, he offers to serve in its place until another canine can be trained, and so becomes known as the 'hound (*cú*) of Culann'. The nickname sticks and he is known as the 'hound of Ulster' when he leads the Red Branch Knights.

Cú Chulainn's capacity as a warrior is greatly increased by the *gáe-bolg*, a magical spear. It is

given to him by Scáthach, his Scottish martial
arts tutor and lover, who teaches him to throw
it with his foot. His sword, *Cailidcheann* ('hard-
headed'), is all but invincible, but his most
terrifying attribute is his ability to put himself
into a *riastrad* (contortion) that distorts his face,
making one eye tiny and the other huge. A deadly
beam of light shoots from the huge eye and
causes blood to burst from his skull. When in
this battle frenzy, he is capable of great slaughter
and does not recover until he is immersed in
three tubs of ice-cold water. Once Conchobar's
wife, Mughain, forces the same transformation
on him when she and the other women of Emain
Macha parade naked in front of him.

Of the many lovers in Cú Chulainn's career,
two are prominent: Emer and Fand. Emer (who
possessed the ideal 'six gifts of womanhood':
beauty, chastity, sweet speech, needlework,
voice and wisdom) becomes his wife, but this

relationship is almost destroyed when Cú Chulainn falls in love with the fairy Fand, the wife of Manannan Mac Lir, the sea god. Fand eventually gives him up when Emer offers to step aside; her magnanimity touches the fairy. Manannan shakes his magical cloak between Fand and Cú Chulainn so they can never meet again, and he also grants Emer and Cú Chulainn the gift of forgetting.

Cú Chulainn sires a son, Conlaí, by Aoife, the sister of Scáthach. Unaware that Aoife is pregnant, he leaves her. Conlaí's aunt teaches the boy the same skills as she taught his father and as a young warrior he goes looking for Cú Chulainn. When Conlaí refuses to identify himself, Cú Chulainn challenges him, in spite of a warning by Emer that the young champion might be his son. As Conlaí lies dying he reveals his identity, to Cú Chulainn's intense sorrow.

Cú Chulainn is most famously associated

with his lone defence of Ulster against the armies of Medb of Connacht, an epic struggle related in the great *Táin Bó Cuailnge*. During the struggle he is forced to kill his closest friend, Ferdia, with the *gáe-bolga* at the relentless Battle of the Ford, said to have taken place at a site near modern Ardee.

As well as mortal enemies, Mórrígán, the goddess of slaughter, pursues Cú Chulainn because he rejects her advances. In the story of his death, the hero is mortally wounded during a battle with the sons of those he has killed and straps himself to a pillar because he wishes to die standing up. It is only when the Mórrígán, in her favourite guise of a crow, perches on his shoulder that his enemies believe he is dead and dare approach. This graphic final scene became the theme for the bronze statue 'The Death of Cúchulainn' (1912) by Oliver Sheppard, now in the General Post Office in Dublin.

MICHAEL CUSACK

Founder of the GAA
1847–1906

MICHAEL CUSACK was born at Carron, on the eastern edge of the Burren, in County Clare in 1847, the darkest year of the Great Famine. Little is known of his early life but he became a teacher, serving for some time as tutor to the family of Lord Gough, and he taught in Enniscorthy (as a pupil teacher at seventeen) and nearer home in Corofin. He qualified as a teacher in Dublin and was the principal of Lough Cutra National School, near Gort in County Galway, from 1866 to 1871. He was on the staff of St Colman's in Newry and later in Blackrock College, Dublin (1874), in St John's College, Kilkenny and finally at Clongowes Wood. He also spent some time in America before settling in Dublin and opening a grind school with a partner, first in North Great George's Street and later in nearby Nelson Street. His Civil Service Academy, in 4 Gardiner Place, to prepare young men for entrance examinations for Trinity College, the Royal College of Surgeons, the navy, army, constabulary and even the civil service, was very successful. With individual tuition as well as the regular classes at the Academy, Cusack managed to earn a regular yearly income of £1,500 a year (more than €112,000 today), impressive considering that he had no friends on the Board of Education and made no secret of his vigorous nationalist ideals.

Sometime before 1880 he married Margaret Woods. He was a striking, bearded figure with broad shoulders, who preferred knee breeches to trousers and always carried a stout blackthorn. The stick he called *Bás-gan-sagart* ('Death without a priest') and it was believed to have been a family relic of the faction fights of his grandfather's time. In later years his dog, a Kerry Blue called Garryowen, always accompanied him.

Cusack tended somewhat to self-introduction, apparently shouting at bartenders, 'I'm Citizen Cusack, from the Parish of Carron in the Barony of Burren in the County of Clare, you Protestant dog!' This has led to his identification with the Citizen in James Joyce's *Ulysses* (1922), the one-eyed essence of narrow-minded nationalism, 'the bare-kneed, brawny-handed, hairy-legged, ruddy-faced, sinewy-armed hero'. There is some debate about whether this attribution is correct, but if it is, it is likely that Joyce, at least, was misled by his extrovert, even noisy demeanour. Cusack's closer friends regarded him as the embodiment of great good humour and no doubt a psychologist would have suggested that the overt bluster was a cover for either timidity or deep insecurity.

Cusack's greatest claim to fame was the part he played in the founding of the Gaelic Athletic Association (GAA) in Hayes Commercial Hotel, Thurles, County Tipperary on 1 November 1884. Acknowledged as a fine athlete himself, and a shot-putt champion, Cusack had been a strong advocate of the 'British' games of cricket and rugby but felt that the control of sport by alien bodies could not be good for Ireland.

One of his co-founders, Maurice Davin from Carrick-on-Suir in County Tipperary, was also a champion athlete, who held many records for running, hurdling, jumping and weight-throwing. Like Cusack, he was conscious that all aspects of games and athletic competitions were run by British bodies and under British rules.

The aim of the Thurles meeting was to establish 'a Gaelic athletic association for the pre-servation and cultivation of national pastimes'. There were not many people at the meeting but they included John Wyse Power, a member of the Irish Republican Brotherhood. (The association of the GAA with the IRB and Fenianism later caused it to be regarded as subversive by the British authorities and suspect by the Catholic Church.) Also present were John McKay, a Belfast man who worked for *The Cork Examiner*; John K. Bracken, a monumental sculptor who was the father of the colourful Brendan Bracken, later Viscount Bracken and a close associate of Winston Churchill; and Thomas St George McCarthy, a district inspector in the Royal Irish Constabulary.

Despite the small number at the inaugural meeting, the association rapidly grew in strength. Cusack was elected secretary, with Wyse Power and McKay as assistants; Davin became the first president. Such was the abrasiveness of Cusack that he was not allowed to retain his post for long and was soon ousted.

The association quickly became a nationalist as well as a cultural rallying point. It soon had patrons whose politics were manifestly anti-British: Charles Stewart Parnell, Michael Davitt and Thomas William Croke, archbishop of Cashel & Emly. Croke was believed to have fought during the 1848 revolution in Paris, where he had studied for the priesthood. The cardinal archbishop of Dublin, Paul Cullen, distrusted both his nationalism and his Gallicanism. It was due to Croke that the GAA became such a success in rural areas and that in its earlier years it was associated with the temperance movement.

Michael Cusack died in 1906. He and Davin are commemorated by the Cusack and Davin stands in Croke Park stadium. This was built on land acquired by the GAA in 1913 and a €250 million redevelopment of the stadium was completed in 2002.

MICHAEL DAVITT

Land League Founder
1846–1906

MICHAEL DAVITT was born in Straide, between Castlebar and Foxford in County Mayo, on 25 March 1846, the second of the five children of Martin and Catherine Davitt. The Great Famine was rising to a cataclysmic crescendo in the year of his birth, and four years later, to add to their misery, the family was evicted. At first they tried the workhouse, but when they realised that male children over three years of age were separated from their mothers, Catherine insisted on emigrating to Lancashire, joining many other Irish people driven from their homes by hunger and laissez-faire economics to a land that did not welcome them, in an attempt to survive. They covered the forty-eight miles from Liverpool to Haslingden, where they found shelter and work, on foot.

On 8 May 1857 a further blow fell when Michael's right arm was so mangled in an accident at the cotton mill where he was working that it had to be amputated. There was no offer of compensation.

Michael's father had some education and when John Dean, a local benefactor, suggested that the lad should attend a local Wesleyan school, he encouraged Michael to accept. Michael later worked for the local postman, who was also a printer, and, in spite of his disability, learned to set type. Soon he was delivering the mail and advancing his education by attending night classes at the local Mechanics Institute, where he first formed his views on land ownership and the possibility of independence for Ireland.

It was almost inevitable that he should join

the Irish Republican Brotherhood (IRB), members of which were commonly known as Fenians. He became organising secretary for England and Scotland. After an unsuccessful Fenian raid on Chester Castle on 11 September 1867, he evaded capture, but was arrested on 14 May 1870 at Paddington Station while awaiting a shipment of arms. He was sentenced to fifteen years' penal servitude and served seven in the dreaded Dartmoor Prison in Devon.

The treatment of Fenian prisoners was particularly cruel. They spent most of their time in solitary confinement, often with their hands manacled behind their backs. Imprisonment gave him plenty of time to study and ponder the Irish land question, and he became convinced that nationalisation of the land was the only possible solution to the problem. Unlike most of the other republican activists, with the exception of James Connolly, his plans for Ireland were socialist in nature. His vision for land-owning had its roots in the economic theories of the American Henry George, based upon a single land tax.

In 1873, while he was in Dartmoor, his mother and three sisters emigrated to Philadelphia. After he was released from Dartmoor on a 'ticket-of-leave' on 19 December 1877, because of agitation in parliament over prison conditions, he arranged to travel to America to see them and to give a series of lectures organised by John Devoy, who effectively controlled Clan na Gael, an Irish-American republican organisation. Whilst there, he managed to get the Irish-Americans to support the Plan of Campaign devised by William O'Brien and other Parnellites, and his own New Departure (a series of Land Acts that compensated landlords and enabled tenants to acquire their holdings), which linked the land agitation with the political campaign for Home Rule.

By the time of Wyndham's Land Act in 1903,

it seemed even to the Irish Parliamentary Party that the problem of landlordism in Ireland had been solved. What had started out as a campaign for the 'Three Fs' (Fair Rent, Fixity of Tenure and Free Sale) had resulted in the virtual return of Irish land to the Irish people. Without Davitt's organisational ability and leadership charisma, the (for him perverted) success of the agrarian reforms would never have been achieved. But he was bitterly disappointed to find that life changed little for the very poor. Those who benefited most from the series of reforming Land Acts were the larger tenant farmers.

Davitt became a world traveller, lecturing on humanitarian issues in most European countries, Australia, New Zealand, South Africa, Palestine and South America, and he crossed the Atlantic like a commuter. In 1886 he married Mary Yore and they had three sons and two daughters. One of their daughters, Kathleen, died of tuberculosis in 1895 aged seven. By then the family was back in Ireland, living in a cottage in Ballybrack in Dalkey, County Dublin, given to Michael and Mary by the people of Ireland as a wedding present.

While in Portland Prison in Britain (February 1881–May 1882), his ticket-of-leave revoked, Davitt had been elected MP for Meath but was disqualified because he was a convict. Ten years later he was returned for North Meath but was unseated after complaints of clerical interference in the election. From 1895 to 1899 he represented South Mayo, resigning in protest against the second Boer War. By then he had lost patience with what he perceived as parliament's inability to make any useful changes in society. He was, however, interested in the formation of the British Labour Party and friendly with its founder, Keir Hardie. But his commitment to the Liberals as the party likely to grant Home Rule was such that he refused to join the new

Labour Party and thus lost the friendship of Hardie, until a rapprochement a year before his death. This support was also to cause him serious conflict with the Catholic Church; he approved of the Liberal policy of state control of education that was anathema to the Church and it was even more concerned about his continuing campaign for nationalisation.

Davitt died of acute septic poisoning on 30 May 1906, in his sixty-first year. In the pre-antibiotic age, this was usually terminal. He had left instructions that there be no public funeral. His body was taken from the Elphis Hospital in Dublin to the Carmelite Friary in Clarendon Street. The lord lieutenant, Lord Aberdeen, attended the removal, an indication of the journey the old Fenian had made. 20,000 people filed past the coffin in Clarendon Street and the body was then taken to Foxford by train and buried in the grounds of Straide Abbey, near his birthplace.

ÉAMON DE VALERA

Revolutionary and Statesman
1882–1975

E DWARD GEORGE DE VALERA (he became Éamon after a self-christening when he joined the Gaelic League in 1908) was born in Manhattan, New York city on 14 October 1882, to Juan Vivion de Valera, a Spanish-Cuban, and Kate Coll from Knockmore in Bruree, County Limerick. His father died when he was two years old and he was sent by his mother to live with his grandmother, Elizabeth Coll, in Knockmore.

He attended the local school at Bruree and later the Christian Brothers School in Charleville, requiring him to walk a total of seven miles each day, since the household could not afford a bicycle. He played rugby at school and later, and his pleasure in the sport remained with him throughout his long life. In 1898, at the age of sixteen, he won a scholarship to Blackrock College, County Dublin. In 1903 he was appointed to the staff as a teacher of mathematics, and in 1904 completed a degree from the Royal University of Ireland. He applied for several university posts without success but finally obtained a post in Carysfort Teacher-Training College for women in Blackrock. He also became a part-time lecturer in Maynooth Seminary.

Though noted for his lack of interest in politics, being anti-republican if anything while at university, his attitude changed when he joined the Gaelic League, and his lifelong dedication to the Irish language became mixed with republican aspirations. He married Sinéad Flanagan, his Gaelic League Irish teacher, on 8 January 1910 in St Paul's church, Arran Quay. The first of their seven children was born in 1911. The

conservative student had become an active republican, joining the Irish Volunteers at its inaugural meeting on 25 November 1913. He joined
the Irish Republican Brotherhood reluctantly
and would not attend meetings, preferring to
carry out his assigned duties as commandant of
the Third Battalion and adjutant of the Dublin
Brigade of the Volunteers. He was involved in
the landing of arms at Howth in July 1914.

During the Easter Rising of 1916 he was
in command of Boland's Mill in Grand Canal
Street, which saw little action. After the surrender, he was the only commander not to be executed. His American citizenship may have played
some part in his reprieve, but more probably he
was saved by timing. Such was the revulsion at
the executions in Britain and elsewhere, that
not even General Sir John Maxwell, the virtual
military dictator, dared risk more criticism by
continuing with them.

Released under the general amnesty in 1917, after incarceration in Dartmoor, Maidstone and Lewes, he was imprisoned again in Lincoln in 1918 because of his vociferous campaign against conscription. He was able to make an impression of the chaplain's master key using candle wax from the prison chapel and a drawing was sent to republicans in Ireland. When copies smuggled into the prison failed to work, blank keys were sent in, from which Peter DeLoughry fashioned a successful copy, and on 3 February de Valera escaped and was taken back to Ireland. Michael Collins was the chief organiser on the outside. These two men could not help but become rivals, because of their widely differing personalities.

De Valera was in America for most of the War of Independence and he deliberately absented himself from the Treaty negotiating team. He campaigned against the Treaty after the Dáil accepted it, thereby hastening a terrible civil war, but did his best to stop the war when he saw the extremes to which both sides were driven. After the death of the IRA's commander-in-chief, Liam Lynch, he wrote the communiqué that required them to lay down their arms. Because of his fervent, even scrupulous, Catholicism he was not happy with violence and he bore the wilderness years after the end of the Civil War with characteristic stoicism. He was also able to get to know his children, whose rearing had been entirely in the hands of Sinéad between 1916 and 1923.

By 1926, realising the uselessness of political abstention, he formed a new party, Fianna Fáil ('Warriors of Ireland'). It had at its head many veterans of 1916, the War of Independence and the Civil War. In 1927 he took the oath of allegiance (the Treaty clause that the anti-Treatyites refused to accept) with metaphorically gritted teeth and entered the Dáil as TD for Clare. The next five years were spent in a masterly process of building up a modern political party that would be true to the goals that all the republicans had fought for. The process included the setting up of a new newspaper, the *Irish Press*, in 1931, intended to reflect governmental views. Some of the money was obtained from the Fianna Fáil faithful by offering them essentially unredeemable shares. Thus the paper could have been said to belong to half the country.

A narrow victory in the general election on 16 February 1932 gave the party seventy-two seats. To try to obtain a majority de Valera called another election on 24 January 1933 and that resulted in seventy-seven seats, an overall majority of one. It was enough and the party held power for sixteen years, during which de Valera's stature as a statesman grew. He was both taoiseach and minister for external affairs, and his appearances at the League of Nations in Geneva greatly enhanced the Free State's reputation internationally.

He was still a gadfly to Britain and by 1937, when his new constitution became law, he had, at great cost to the ordinary people of the country, begun an economic war by introducing prohibitive tariffs on British goods. He removed all imperial and royal emblems, dismissing the remnants of the old regime, including the office of governor-general. He took the Treaty ports back from the Royal Navy and, against great British and US pressure, held on to them during the Second World War, resolutely maintaining Éire's (as the country was known after 1937) neutrality, though with less steeliness towards the Allies than the Axis countries. (He famously sent fire crews to help during the air raids on Belfast.)

His social and economic policy was based on the papal encyclicals, *Rerum Novarum* (1891) and *Quadragesimo Anno* (1931). He was much quoted (and mocked) after a speech on St Patrick's Day 1943 aspiring to a country that 'would be joyous with the romping of sturdy children, the contests of athletic youths and the laughter of comely maidens'. But his answer to Winston Churchill, after a talk filled with post-war bluster disrespecting Ireland's independence, gained him much support at home and abroad:

Mr Churchill makes it clear that, in certain circumstances, he would have violated our neutrality and that he would justify his action by Britain's necessity. It seems strange to me that Mr Churchill does not see that this, if accepted, would mean Britain's necessity would become a moral code and that when this necessity became sufficiently great, other people's rights were not to count … Surely

Mr Churchill must see that if his contention be admitted in our regard, a like justification can be framed for similar acts of aggression elsewhere and no small nation adjoining a great power could ever hope to be permitted to go its own way in peace …

Mr Churchill is proud of Britain's stand alone, after France had fallen and before America entered the War. Could he not find in his heart the generosity to acknowledge that there is a small nation that stood alone not for one year or two, but for several hundred years against aggression; that endured spoliations, famines, massacres in endless succession; that was clubbed many times into insensibility, but that each time on returning consciousness took up the fight anew; a small nation that could never be got to accept defeat and has never surrendered her soul? … we shall go on and strive to play our part in the world continuing unswervingly to work for the cause of true freedom and for peace and understanding.

The influence of John Charles McQuaid, arch-bishop of Dublin from 1940, upon de Valera was regarded by detractors as immoderate, but correspondence of ideas was mistaken for clerical interference; de Valera was really too strong a character to be affected.

He was only out of office twice between 1932 and his retirement in 1959, and served as president from then until 1973, the maximum two terms. His eyesight had troubled him since 1936 and in spite of several operations, he was left with only peripheral vision from 1952. He died on 29 August 1975 after a remarkable career but with two of his greatest ambitions unfulfilled: the restoration of the Irish language and the ending of the partition of his country.

MADELEINE
FFRENCH-MULLEN
&
KATHLEEN LYNN

Revolutionaries and Humanitarians
1880–1944 & 1874–1955

KATHLEEN FLORENCE LYNN and
Madeleine Ffrench-Mullen were close
friends and fellow revolutionaries whose lives
and careers were inextricably linked after their
first meeting as members of the Irish Citizen
Army (ICA) in 1913.

Kathleen was the elder by six years, having
been born on 28 January 1874 in Mallaghfarry,
near Killala in County Mayo, the daughter of
Canon Robert Lynn and his wife. The family
later moved to Cong. Even as a child Kathleen

was aware of the poverty in the country. She was educated at Alexandra College for girls in Dublin, noted for its liberal feminism and advocacy of women's suffrage. It gave her the courage and impetus to become a doctor against a lot of informal male and establishment opposition, and she graduated from the Royal University in 1899. (An example of the climate at the time is the case of Frances Hegarty, who in 1906 appeared to sit a final Arts examination and entered the hall as the only woman. There was consternation at her presence, caused by the misprinting of her name as Francis. The invigilator could not dismiss her because her papers were there but he surrounded her with screens to shield her from male eyes – or vice versa!)

Even as an undergraduate, Kathleen had shown great medical skill, winning the Barker Anatomical Prize from the Royal College of Surgeons, a distinction 'not hitherto achieved by a woman'. Although her appointment to the staff of the Adelaide Hospital was rejected because of male opposition, she 'walked the wards' in Holles Street (1897–99), the Rotunda (1899), the Royal Victoria Eye and Ear Hospital (1902–16) and the Richmond Lunatic Asylum. She also spent some time in America achieving a further medical qualification and had the distinction of being the first woman resident in the Eye and Ear Hospital. In 1904 she set up in private practice at 9 Belgrave Road, Rathmines and in 1909 was awarded a Fellowship of the Royal College of Surgeons.

Over time Kathleen became increasingly concerned about the condition of the Dublin poor, which was exacerbated by the lockout of 1913. She began to believe that only by direct action could any improvement be made in the poverty-racked Ireland of the time. Active in relief work for the hungry children of the locked-out workers, she also joined the ICA, set up by James Connolly in 1913 to defend demonstrating workers and pickets against the often violent attacks of the Dublin Metropolitan Police, who were used as strike breakers. She provided the members of the ICA with first-aid lessons.

Madeleine Ffrench-Mullen was born in Malta in 1880, the eldest child of St Laurence Ffrench-Mullen, a fleet surgeon in the Royal Navy stationed on the island. On his retirement, the family returned to Ireland and Madeleine began to take an interest in the condition of the Dublin poor. She was one of the first members of Inghinidhe na hÉireann ('The Daughters of Ireland'), founded by Maud Gonne in 1900. It was a revolutionary body that grew out of the Patriotic Children's

Treat Committee, which had shown both its militant and its humanitarian sides when the members, spurred on by Madeleine, organised a treat for 30,000 schoolchildren in deliberate opposition to the event arranged in Phoenix Park to mark the official visit of the eighty-one-year-old Queen Victoria (1819–1901).

The actress Helena Molony, also a member of Inghinidhe na hÉireann, began a magazine called *Bean na hÉireann* (*The Irishwoman*), which advocated 'complete separatism, the rising cause of feminism and the interests of Irish women generally'. Madeleine wrote the children's column for the magazine using the names 'Dectora' (Cú Chulainn's mother) and 'M. O'Callaghan'. Inghinidhe na hÉireann, against much opposition, advocated free school dinners and inevitably drew down the disapproval of the Catholic Church.

It was natural that Madeleine should take

part in the lockout agitation. She worked in the soup kitchen in Liberty Hall, the ITGWU's headquarters. It was during this period that she met Dr Lynn, who was giving a lecture on first aid, and they became lifelong friends.

During Easter Week 1916 Kathleen was sent as chief surgeon to the garrison at City Hall under the command of Seán Connolly and his lieutenant John O'Reilly, but when both were killed she took command and negotiated the surrender on Tuesday 25 April. She informed the startled officer who took the surrender that she was a Red Cross doctor, but insisted that she was also a 'belligerent' and an active member of the ICA. After her surrender she was held in Ship Street Barracks, Richmond Barracks, Kilmainham Gaol and eventually Mountjoy Prison, before being deported to England, where she was allowed to continue her medical work under supervision.

Madeleine was with the main ICA force in St

Stephen's Green during the Rising and they soon found it necessary to retreat to the Royal College of Surgeons building as the Green was under fire from the Shelbourne Hotel. As a lieutenant, she had fifteen women under her command; their duties consisted of the commandeering of vehicles, the evacuation of civilians and tending the wounded. On the afternoon of Wednesday 26 April she tried to persuade some of the women in the college to try to make their way home, but they refused to desert their posts. She was arrested when the garrison, somewhat belatedly, followed Pearse's order to surrender. She was taken to Kilmainham and later transferred to Mountjoy until her release on 4 July.

Kathleen, who returned to Ireland in August 1916, became a member of the newly constituted Sinn Féin in 1917 and is remembered for the heroic work she did for those suffering during the influenza pandemic of 1918. Though active in the War of Independence, her most obvious contribution to society was the founding, with Madeleine, of St Ultan's Hospital (*Teach Ultáin*) for sick infants in Charlemont Street in 1919. They started with less than £100 and two cots. For a while they had a policy of appointing only women to the staff. At the time, infant mortality was running at 150 per thousand births. The two women pioneered the use of the BCG vaccination against tuberculosis, then endemic, and, impressed by the educational theories of Maria Montessori, established a Montessori ward at St Ultan's.

The partners continued their social work outside of the hospital, enduring the longueurs of local government politics in order to facilitate the building of decent apartments for slum dwellers. Kathleen had been elected to Dáil Éireann in 1923 as a Sinn Féin TD but did not take her seat because of the party's abstentionist policy.

Dismayed by Sinn Féin's lack of coherent social policy, she left politics a few years later.

Madeleine died in 1944, aged sixty-four, but Kathleen continued her social and medical work until her death on 14 September 1955 at St Mary's, an Anglican care home in Dublin.

GRANUAILE

'A Most Famous Feminine Sea-Captain'
c. 1530–1603

GRANUAILE, though a real historical character, is the heroine of a body of myth of
the kind that inevitably attaches itself to a character from her period of history, as venturesome,
courageous and unorthodox as she was. Even the
name by which she is known is problematic: the
fanciful suggestion that it comes from the Irish
Gráinne Mhaol ('Bald Grace') is unlikely to be
true, though it fits well with the legend that she
wore her hair as short as a man's. Storytellers may
have assumed it practical that she removed the
female burdens of long hair and cumbersome
skirts when she roved the west coast of Ireland,
an area that she insisted was her bailiwick.

The anglicised version of her name is probably taken from Gráinne Ní Mháille, her name in Irish or, less likely, from Gráinne Umhaill, 'Grace of Umhall', from the name of her family's lands, which included many islands in and around Clew Bay in County Mayo. Her stronghold was Clare Island, at the entrance to the island-rich inlet, protected by Achill to the north and by Inishbofin to the south. Clare Island is taken as the place of her birth and tradition has her buried there as well.

She was 'a most famous feminine sea-captain' in the words of one of her adversaries, Lord Deputy Sir Henry Sidney, the first deputy of Ireland for Elizabeth I. Her people were sea rovers, a polite name for pirates, though the greater part of their illegal activities was commercial. The nearest port was Galway but during Granuaile's life it was a kind of independent city-state run by Old English merchants loyal to the Tudor crown, who had accepted English sovereignty and cooperated in their rationalisation of native Irish nobility known as 'Surrender and Regrant'. The O'Malleys, forbidden the use of the port because of their insistence on the primacy of Brehon law, traded with Scotland, France and Spain, all enemies of England, and were deemed traitorous. Since they were cut off from normal mercantile processes, they imposed their own excise duty on passing vessels they captured.

Granuaile was born around 1530 and took to the sea as naturally as a dolphin. The O'Malley family motto, *Terra Marique Potens* ('Powerful by land and sea'), was certainly exemplified in her life. Her father was Dubhdara ('Black Oak') O'Malley, who married Margaret O'Malley from another branch of the clan. Her assumed aristocracy was partly familial and partly obtained by two dynastic marriages. Her father had been accepted as lord of that part of the coast by local approval and Brehon law, and so Granuaile regarded herself as a princess.

When she was fifteen she married Dónal an Cogaidh ('warring Daniel') O'Flaherty of Bally-nahinch in Connemara, one of the 'ferocious' O'Flahertys. She bore him two sons, Owen and Murrough, and a daughter, Margaret, who dis-appointed her mother by being too sweet and feminine. Dónal was killed in a tribal dispute with another of the Galway tribes, the Joyces, and Granuaile continued the struggle, eventually capturing the Joyces' stronghold, termed locally Caisleán an Choiligh (Cock's Castle); after that it was known throughout Connacht as Caisleán na Circe ('Hen's Castle').

The story goes that her second marriage, to Risteárd an Iarainn de Burca ('Iron Dick' Burke) in 1566, lasted just one year, after which, as permitted by Brehon law, she divorced him, by peremptorily rejecting him from the battlements of Rockfleet Castle, his own fortress, near New-port, County Mayo. It was known in Irish as Carraig an Chabhlaigh ('The Rock of the Fleet') and it served as the last link in the protective chain with which she felt it necessary to surround her domain. However, state papers show that, officially at least, she remained married to Richard until his death.

The marriage resulted in another son, appropriately named Tiobóid na Long ('Theobald of the Ships'), who, according to the legend, was born at sea when his mother was thirty-seven. The day after his birth she successfully defeated an attack on her ship by Algerian pirates. By then she had mustered a band of 200 rovers to help her and she was unbiased about her selection of targets, but a substantial majority proved to be English. The English administration in Dublin had both the means and will to stop her 'piracy'. They were utterly ruthless in imposing English 'civility' and although she successfully repulsed an English attack on Rockfleet in 1574, she was taken prisoner three years later and imprisoned in Dublin Castle for eighteen months.

In 1584 Sir Richard Bingham, the new governor of Connacht, became her implacable enemy, arresting her, confiscating her land and properties, killing her son Owen and 'turning' Murrough.

It was about this time that the most persistent of the legends about Granuaile began. It is claimed that she insisted on petitioning Queen Elizabeth, travelling to London in 1593 for a meeting of majesties. They met, it is said, at Greenwich and the Irish pirate would not kneel; she, too, was a queen. Their secret conversation was in Latin – Grace as a member of the Irish nobility would have had an appropriate education – and she offered to 'invade with sword and fire all your highness' enemies'. As a result of the meeting, her son Tiobóid was granted the title

Viscount of Mayo and Grace was pardoned from any charges of treason.

However Bingham continued to persecute her, eventually driving her to seek refuge with Thomas, Earl of Ormond, in Munster. When Bingham was removed from his post in 1596 she returned to Clare Island, but little is known about the last part of her life. She and the other queen both died in 1603; Elizabeth is buried in Westminster Abbey, the 'famous feminine sea captain' in a grave on Clare Island.

With the sense that she was essentially unconquered, the name of Granuaile became associated with Ireland's long struggle for freedom. She has featured in song and story, and modern Irish women have hailed her as a feminist icon.

HENRY GRATTAN

Patriot and Orator
1746–1820

HENRY GRATTAN was born in Dublin on 3 July 1746, the son of James, the recorder for the city and its MP between 1761 and 1765. He and his father were much at odds, mainly because of James' conservative views about the relationship of the Irish parliament to that of Britain and Henry's stubborn resistance to his father's plan to make him a lawyer. He studied Classics at Trinity and, acquiescing briefly to his father's wishes, attended the Middle Temple in London from 1767. He was called to the Irish bar in 1772 but rarely practised. Instead he came under the patronage of Henry Flood, who was a 'patriot' – one of the party who wished to end

Ireland's economic dependency on Great Britain – and was introduced to the circle of what we might call nationalists, though Grattan came late to the support of Catholic emancipation and Flood was firmly against it.

In 1775, just at the start of the American revolution, Grattan was given the safe seat of Charlemont in Armagh by the earl of the same name and stunned the Commons with his rhetorical ability. Around this time Grattan also became the parliamentary leader of the patriots, when Flood injudiciously accepted the government office of vice-treasurer of Ireland, severely damaging his reputation with the Irish.

In 1779–80 Grattan began an oratorical campaign for free trade, and for the repeal of Poynings Law (1494) and the Declaratory Act (1720), known popularly as the 'sixth of George I', which gave the British parliament the right to pass laws for Ireland.

When the conservative British government of Lord North fell in 1782 because of the debacle of the American War of Independence, the new, but short-lived Whig prime minister, Lord Rockingham, in one of his last acts, repealed these laws which had rendered the Irish parliament little more than a talking shop. Grattan's impassioned oratory played a large part in this achievement, as did pressure from the Irish Volunteers, a Protestant militia which had been set up in Ireland

to replace the British soldiers sent to fight the war in America in case of an attack by France. For the next eighteen years, until the Act of Union, the Irish parliament was known as 'Grattan's Parliament'.

The newly liberated parliament showed its gratitude by declaring Grattan a national hero and awarding him £50,000 (about €4.7 million today). He was offered £100,000 but would accept only half that amount.

The Irish parliament was essentially that of the Anglican Anglo-Irish; it was a Protestant parliament that Catholics played no part in. Presbyterians, though never as deprived as Catholics, were also excluded from the parliament. Despite the Ascendancy bias, a few relief acts were passed in 1782 to improve the lot of Catholics. A further act in 1793 removed most of the penal exclusions imposed at the beginning of the century, leaving only one final hurdle for full

Catholic emancipation: the ability to be elected to parliament. Grattan's attempt to bring in a bill offering a diluted form of Catholic emancipation was defeated in 1795.

The period of Grattan's parliament was marked by a number of serious events, two of which – the regency crisis of 1788–89 and the rising of 1798 – were of major concern to the conservative Westminster government led by William Pitt the Younger. In 1788, when George III succumbed to one of his recurring bouts of illness, Grattan, anxious to please Charles James Fox and his Whigs (and not at all displeased to oppose Pitt), strongly supported the move to make the king's eldest son Prince Regent. The prince was pleased at this Irish support and the wider powers which Grattan would have granted him. The crisis passed when the king recovered, but Grattan had made an enemy of Pitt, who resolved to obliterate the rogue Irish parliament.

The beginning of the French Revolution in 1789 stirred the minds of those already elated by the success of the American colonies in setting up a confederation independent of Britain to consider a revolutionary solution to the stagnation of politics in Ireland. They were not impressed by the illusory suggestion that the new regime had brought a kind of golden age, and younger men such as Wolfe Tone and Henry Joy McCracken decided to emulate in a smaller way the *sansculottes* who caused the fall of the Bastille and eventually the *Ancien Régime*. In 1791 the Society of the United Irishmen was formed to push for reform and in 1798 it led a rising against British rule. The rising had little support, however, and was put down with extreme cruelty by mainly Anglican militias, with support from the tolerated Orange Order.

Following this rising the British government decided to impose union by force or, preferably, by bribery. Paradoxically, the union was supported by the Catholic Church and its members due to the promise of emancipation, and bitterly opposed by the Established Church. The struggle produced one of Grattan's greatest speeches: 'Yet I do not give up the country; I see her in a swoon, but she is not dead. Though in her tomb she lies helpless and motionless, still there is on her lips the spirit of life, and on her cheek a glow of beauty.' He spoke more wisely than he knew.

After the Act of Union (1 January 1801), Grattan was not surprised when Britain once again broke her promise to the Catholics. Although in poor health, he agreed to be elected to the safe seat for Dublin City in 1805. In 1819 his health began to fail, but he still felt it his duty to attend the Westminster parliament. In May 1820 he sailed from Dublin to Liverpool but could not face the jolting coach journey to London. Instead, his last journey was made slowly and with some dignity by canal, and he died on 4 June in London. He is buried in Westminster Abbey, near his enemy Pitt and his friend Fox, and a statue of him stands in the outer lobby of the House of Commons – both tributes to the esteem in which he was held by the British parliament. Another statue, by John Henry Foley, stands in the middle of College Green, Dublin.

BETSY GRAY

Insurgent
c. 1778–1798

BETSY GRAY has attracted so much local lore that it is hard to detach the well-intended fiction of the repeated folktales that have adhered to her legend from the cold, hard facts. A few things are certain: she was born in County Down, took part in the battle of Ballynahinch and perished afterwards.

The subject of many local ballads and fireside stories in her native county, Betsy became known province-wide when in 1888 Wesley Guard Lyttle published a serialised novel in the *North Down Herald,* of which he was editor, called *Betsy Gray or Hearts of Down: A Tale of Ninety-Eight*. It was written in highly dramatic nineteenth-century prose with a dusting of County Down dialect, and became immensely popular. It was found on many rustic bookshelves beside the Bible and the works of Burns, which, considering the bawdy nature of some of the poems ascribed to him, always seems an odd juxtaposition. Usually, those same houses also had a framed print of the heroine on her white horse brandishing a sword as she charged the troops of General Nugent at Ballynahinch.

According to Lyttle, she was born 'where six roads unite in the townland of Granshaw (a common place name in Ireland since it connotes a farmstead) in the County of Down, at a point two and a half miles from Bangor, three miles from Donaghadee and a like distance from Newtownards'. Although Lyttle places her birthplace at Six Road Ends, and asserts that her widowed father, Hans Gray, was a sturdy farmer there, other villages also claim her. Some insist that she was really from Tullyniskey, between Dromara and Waringsford, still in County Down and closer to Ballynahinch, but twenty-six miles at least from the alternative. A house near Waringsford is still pointed out as her birthplace, and her parents are named as John and Rebecca Gray. However, Mary Ann McCracken, the sister of Henry Joy, and an unofficial historian of the 1798 rising, suggested that Betsy was from Killinchy. Mary Ann supplied Richard Robert Madden, one of the earliest chroniclers of the rebellion, with much first-hand information for his seven-volume *The United Irishmen: Their Lives and Times*. Killinchy is close to Strangford Lough, fifteen miles east of Dromara and thirteen south of Six Road Ends. One of Betsy's biographers, Jack McCoy, in his study *Ulster's Joan of Arc* (1987), even goes so far as to ask of her: 'maid or made-up?'

Wherever she was born, her date of birth was

probably around the year 1778, and by the time she was in her teens she must have been aware of the unrest being generated by members of the United Irishmen. While the society's leadership was mostly Presbyterian, marginalised politically and strongly influenced by the American and French revolutions, as time went on a growing number of those who joined were Catholic. Their support for the French led to them being proscribed and forced underground.

In late 1796 the French launched an unsuccessful invasion of Ireland in support of the United Irishmen. The response of the British government was the strict enforcement of the Insurrection Act brought in earlier that year, which gave their commander in Ulster, General Gerard Lake, blanket permission to put down sedition by any means. He was aided in his mission, which involved indiscriminate floggings, burnings and killing, by members of the county yeomanries, many of whom were members of the recently formed Orange Order. On 14 October 1797 an Antrim farmer called William Orr was hanged at Carrickfergus for administering the United Irishmen's oath to two soldiers (who may have been British informants); after this, open insurrection became inevitable.

Betsy, twenty years of age, was not a member of the United Irishmen but her brother, George, and her lover, Willie Boal, were. According to Lyttle, her father wanted her to be brought up as a lady, sending her to a school and making sure that she was not required to do farm work or even household jobs. In spite of this, she interested herself in the insurrection, helping Willie and George to rescue Colonel Bryson of the United Irishmen from imprisonment in Newtownards. They then moved south to Ballynahinch, about fifteen miles from Belfast, to join Henry Munro's force, which had gathered at Monalto, near the town. On 13

June Munro, a Lisburn weaver, led an attack on the forces of General Nugent at Ballynahinch.

Tradition makes a kind of Joan of Arc out of Betsy, as the contemporary prints where she is dressed in green and riding her white charger against the vicious Monaghan militia, chasing them through the centre of Ballynahinch, show. During the battle Nugent's forces were actually withdrawing, but the insurgents did not realise this and, because of a breakdown in communication, they retreated in disarray.

Betsy and her small party fled towards Lisburn in an attempt to make their way home. They had moved less than two miles up the road when a party of the Hillsborough yeomanry intercepted them at a junction with Horner's Road. George and Willie were killed on the spot but Betsy fought on until a man called Jack Gill cut off her gloved sword-hand with his sabre, while Thomas Nelson from Annahilt, a village halfway between

Hillsborough and Ballynahinch, shot her through the eye. James Little, Nelson's neighbour, stripped her and left the three bodies lying on the road. They were discovered there by local farmers and buried at nearby Ballycreen. The grave was marked with a column of black oak.

In 1896 James Gray of Tullyniskey erected a monument at the grave with the terse inscription: 'Elizabeth Gray, George Gray, William Boal, 13 June 1798' and it became a place of nationalist pilgrimage. Just two years later, during the centenary celebrations for 1798, local Orangemen destroyed the shrine, thereby fulfilling the stanza from one of the many Betsy ballads:

> No tombstone marks the grave
> Near the road to Lisburn Town
> And never a spade disturbs the spot
> Where sleeps the hearts of Down.

DOUGLAS HYDE

Gaelic Scholar and First President of Ireland
1860–1949

DOUGLAS HYDE (or Dubhglas de hÍde) was born on 17 January 1860 in Longford House in Castlerea, County Roscommon, where his mother was briefly staying. His father was the Church of Ireland rector of Kilmactranny, County Sligo from 1852 until 1867, when the family moved to Tibohine near Frenchpark in County Roscommon. Hyde was educated at home but learned Irish, as Yeats put it, 'from the company of old countrymen'. Among many other characteristics, he possessed a near-genius capacity for assimilating languages and by the time he became an undergraduate had become fluent in Greek, Latin, Hebrew, German and Irish. He learned his Irish mainly from Seamus Hart and Biddy Crummy, whose little bog hut he visited regularly as a boy and from whom he first heard the words and tune of *Mo Bhrón ar an Bhfarraige* ('My Grief on the Sea'). He included his own translation of this in *Love Songs of Connacht* (1893).

When Hyde went to Trinity College in 1880 he had already published some poems, mainly in Irish, in the *Shamrock* and the *Irishman*, using the pseudonym *An Craoibhín Aoibhinn* ('The charming little branch'). Content to follow in the family tradition and become a clergyman, in 1881 he won the Bedell Scholarship for divinity students who could preach in Irish. (This was established in honour of William Bedell, the Anglican bishop who had arranged for the Bible to be translated into Irish.) But at age twenty-six he had second thoughts about the Church and transferred to the law department, graduating that same year. He continued to work in Irish and published *Leabhar Sgéulaigheachta* (1889), a collection of stories, rhymes and riddles in Irish collected by him in Connacht, and *Beside the Fire* (1890), a collection of folktales with translations. He spent 1891 as professor of modern languages at the University of New Brunswick. He enjoyed the experience and relished the outdoor activities that were such a part of Canadian life. He used the opportunity to visit America and called upon, among others, the old Fenian O'Donovan Rossa.

On 25 November 1892, after his return to Ireland, Hyde gave a revolutionary address to the National Literary Society, of which he became president, entitled 'The Necessity of De-Anglicising Ireland'. He would have known how inflammatory this topic was. His words could be interpreted as subversive and he must have realised that his call for the Irish people to achieve what he called *dhíShacanú* (de-Anglicisation) '*tríd an gceol, trí na cluíchí náisiúnta, ach go mhórmhór tríd an teanga, agus tré labhairt na teanga*' ('through the music, through national games, but especially through the language and through speaking the language'), as he put it in his autobiographical book *Mise agus an Conradh* (1931) ('The League and I'), was essentially a challenge to British rule in Ireland.

On 31 July 1893 Hyde chaired the first meeting of the Gaelic League (*Conradh na Gaeilge*), of which he was co-founder, in O'Kelly's Rooms, 9 Lower O'Connell Street, Dublin. Over the years this organisation, founded with the aim of restoring the Irish language, grew in efficiency and popularity. Teachers were found in the Gaeltacht, where Irish was the first language, and Irish summer colleges trained non-Irish-speaking teachers and adults who regarded the learning of the old language as education.

Hyde already knew W. B. Yeats and in 1898 he met Lady Augusta Gregory, who taught him the elements of dramaturgy. The result was his *Casadh an tSúgáin* ('The Twisting of the Rope'), the first play staged in Irish – except for a few scenes written by Alice Milligan about St Patrick – which was presented in the Gaiety Theatre in Dublin on 21 October 1901, with Hyde himself playing the boastful Munster poet Red Hanrahan. *Pleusgadh na Bulgóide; or The Bursting of the Bubble*, his bilingual satire pillorying the enemies of Irish at Trinity, was presented in the Molesworth Hall on 3 November 1903.

Hyde continued to publish anthologies and critical works about Irish, producing *Love Songs of Connacht* in 1893, the year of his marriage to Lucy Cometina Kurtz. *The Story of Early Gaelic Literature* followed in 1895 and his magisterial *A Literary History of Ireland* (1899) eventually made it possible for Irish to become a compulsory entrance subject at University College Dublin (UCD), as the Royal University was called from 1909. He held the post as professor of Modern Irish at that university from 1909 until his retirement in 1932.

In 1915 Hyde relinquished the chairmanship of the Gaelic League because he could see that it had become politicised, and was replaced by the other co-founder, Eoin MacNeill.

He served as a member of the senate from 1909, but when membership of the upper house became elective in 1925 his candidacy was opposed by a strong campaign from the Catholic Truth Society, who made a number of untrue charges based upon his support of divorce, probably because of his Protestantism, and he failed to be elected.

Seemingly unperturbed, he retired from public life, moving between UCD and his home in Ratra, near Frenchpark. He and his wife had two daughters, Nuala and Una. Nuala died of tuberculosis in 1916, while his wife, Lucy, died in 1938.

In 1938 Hyde became the first president of Ireland (under the 1937 constitution). His election was an all-party affair and his term was uncontroversial. In 1940 he suffered a serious stroke, which he survived, though he was partially paralysed. He resigned from office on 24 June 1945 but was too weak to return to Ratra. Instead, he was accommodated in what had been the residence of the lord lieutenant's secretary in Dublin, where he died on 12 July 1949. His state funeral was notable in that Catholic members of the Dáil were prohibited by their religion from attending the service in the St Patrick's Church of Ireland cathedral. Hyde is remembered by, among other memorials, the Douglas Hyde Gallery in Trinity, the Hyde Museum in Frenchpark and Dr Hyde GAA Park, Roscommon.

LIAM LYNCH

Republican Commander
1893–1923

LIAM LYNCH was born on 9 November 1893 at the foot of the Galtee Mountains in Barnagurraha, County Limerick, the son of Mary (née Kelly) and Jeremiah Lynch. He was educated at Anglesborough National School, and apprenticed to the hardware business of Messrs O'Neill in nearby Mitchelstown, just over the Cork border. He later went to work in Fermoy with Barry's timber merchants. Lynch's great-grandfather had taken part in the United Irishmen rising of 1798 and he was active in all aspects of Irish nationalism from an early age, joining the Gaelic League and the Ancient Order of Hibernians.

With Sinn Féin's overwhelming general election victory in December 1918, it became clear that a fight for independence was imminent. In 1919 Lynch reorganised and became commandant of Cork No. 2 Brigade of the IRA. On 7 September they attacked a party of the King's Shropshire Light Infantry which was heading for church in Fermoy. Eighteen soldiers were overpowered and thirteen rifles loaded onto waiting cars, and when the military pursued the perpetrators, they found the roads blocked by felled trees. One British soldier died in the attack.

In June 1920 Lynch was one of the party that kidnapped and held the British Brigadier-General Lucas for a month. The IRA served as a local police force in many areas and Lynch later captured three bank robbers, recovering £20,000, which he coolly returned to the bank. Sinn Féin courts gave the miscreants terms of deportation.

In August 1920 the British authorities raided

Cork City Hall and arrested Lynch and others, including Lord Mayor Terence MacSwiney. However, Lynch gave a false name and was released three days later. The British later assassinated two men called Lynch, mistaking them for Liam.

In September 1920 Lynch and Ernie O'Malley, who had been sent by Michael Collins from Dublin to Cork to help with training, planned a successful raid on the British Army barracks in Mallow. They captured thirty rifles and two Hotchkiss machine guns. Reprisals by the Black and Tans wiped out half the town, destroying Protestant and Catholic property indiscriminately. Such reprisals inevitably followed IRA actions.

The War of Independence was characterised by courage and determination, so there was an inevitable sense of deflation over the terms of the Treaty signed in December 1921 which brought an end to the conflict. Lynch felt the 'betrayal' keenly, finding the degeneration of the 1916

Republic into the dominion status offered by the British a mockery of all that the Irish had risked. He was not the only one and the IRA quickly split into pro- and anti-Treaty factions. In March 1922 Lynch became chief of staff of the anti-Treaty IRA.

Despite his opposition to the Treaty, Lynch disapproved of the takeover of the Four Courts by a group of anti-Treaty IRA men led by Rory O'Connor and Liam Mellows. But when the National Army began to shell the Four Courts in June 1922, he threw his support behind these men and returned to Cork to lead the fight against the pro-Treaty Provisional Government and its army. After the defeat of the anti-Treatyites in Dublin, and knowing that his greatest strength lay in the south-west, he determined to set up an independent 'Munster Republic', with a boundary running from Waterford to Limerick. It was intended to include Waterford, Carrick-on-Suir, Clonmel, Fethard, the Golden Vale and Tipperary, with Lynch's headquarters in Limerick – his home ground.

The anti-Treaty forces were quickly over-whelmed by the superior numbers and arma-ments of the National Army. On 20 July 1922 Limerick fell to the Free State forces and Lynch fell back to Fermoy. The 'Munster Republic' was dissolved when the National Army arrived by sea in Cork and Kerry in early August. Effectively surrounded, Lynch reverted to what he was best at: guerrilla tactics.

The war deepened in bitterness and 'fright-fulness' and Lynch sanctioned the killing of TDs, senators, judges and editors who supported the government. The overt reason for this escalation, apparently at odds with Lynch's previous temperament, was the execution of four anti-Treatyites – James Fisher, Peter Cassidy, John F. Gaffney and Richard Twohig – on 17 November, and Erskine Childers on 24 November. The IRA responded with the killing of Seán Hales, TD, on 7 December, which the government matched with the execution of four prisoners: Rory O'Connor, Liam Mellows, Richard Barrett and Joe McKelvey. There followed a series of reprisals on both sides that were more vicious than the worst atrocities of the War of Independence. Seventy official executions of IRA prisoners were carried out and at least 150 'unofficial' ones, although some of these may have been the result of age-old local animosities. IRA responses included the killing of the father of Minister for Justice Kevin O'Higgins and the seven-year-old son of James McGarry, TD.

By early 1923 most senior members of the IRA, including Éamon de Valera, knew that the Civil War was lost. But Lynch was adamant about carrying on and, at a meeting of the executive council in March, argued for the fight to continue. Then, on 10 April 1923, he was fatally wounded in a fight with government forces in the Knockmealdown Mountains in County Tipperary, dying that same day. Just three weeks later Frank Aiken, the new chief of staff of the anti-Treatyites, declared a ceasefire, and on 24 May ordered the dumping of arms. A communiqué issued by de Valera read: 'Soldiers of the Republic, Legion of the Rearguard … Military victory must be allowed to rest for the moment with those who have destroyed the Republic.'

Lynch was buried in Kilcrumper graveyard, near Fermoy. On 7 April 1935 a 60-foot round tower on the spot where he fell in Tipperary was dedicated to him.

TERENCE MacSWINEY
&
TOMÁS MacCURTÁIN

Revolutionaries
1879–1920 & 1884–1920

TERENCE MacSWINEY (aka Toirdhealbhach Mac Suibhne) was born in Cork on 28 March 1879 and educated at North 'Mon' (North Monastery school). Leaving school at age fifteen, he joined a firm of accountants, Dwyer & Co., but continued to study and did a degree at Queen's College, Cork. Though appointed as a commercial teacher and class organiser for County Cork, his passion was for literature and drama. He joined with the nationalist Daniel Corkery in forming the Cork Dramatic Society, for which he wrote several plays based on Celtic mythology;

The Revolutionist (published by Maunsel in Dublin in 1914), with its theme of patriotic self-sacrifice, may now be seen as prophetic. He also wrote poetry, and published and largely wrote the 'journal for militant Ireland', *Fianna Fáil* ('Ireland's warriors'), eleven issues in all, from September 1914 until its suppression in December of that year. He was second-in-command of the Cork Volunteers at their founding in 1913 and president of the Cork branch of Sinn Féin.

MacSwiney's name is often associated with Tomás MacCurtáin, who was commandant of the Irish Volunteers in Cork at the time of the 1916 Rising. MacCurtáin was born in Ballyknockane, County Cork on 20 March 1884 and he, like MacSwiney, attended North 'Mon'. He joined the Blackpool branch of the Gaelic League in Cork in 1901 and became secretary a year later. Joining Sinn Féin in 1906 and the Irish Republican Brotherhood (IRB) in 1907, he also helped run the Cork division of Fianna Éireann, the nationalist youth movement after it was set up in 1911. He contributed to MacSwiney's *Fianna Fáil* and like him, obeyed Eoin MacNeill's order to stand down in Easter Week 1916, though both men had quite some difficulty in persuading the local Volunteers to conform. Both were arrested in the blanket swoop that followed the Rising and held in Wakefield, Frongoch and Reading. They were released under the general amnesty in December 1916. Once home, they became involved in the reorganisation of the Volunteers.

In the municipal elections in 1920, Mac-Curtáin was elected councillor for Cork City's NW Ward No. 3 and chosen to be lord mayor for the city. In his short time as mayor he made several important reforms in the city, but on 20 March he was shot dead in his own house, in front of his wife, by an armed gang in civilian clothes with blackened faces. The coroner's inquest into his death returned a verdict of wilful murder against British Prime Minister David Lloyd George, the lord lieutenant, the chief secretary, the acting inspector-general of the RIC, Divisional Inspector Oswald Swanzy of the RIC and some unknown members of the police force.

In contrast the authorities claimed that the assailants were members of the IRB, impatient with MacCurtáin's apparent inaction in the War of Independence, but no one believed this. When Swanzy, who may have ordered the attack, was on leave in Lisburn, he was shot on 22 August by members of the Cork Volunteers, as legend has it, using MacCurtáin's personal revolver.

MacCurtáin's post as lord mayor of Cork was then taken over by MacSwiney.

MacSwiney had been interned from February 1917, first in Shrewsbury and later at Bromyard internment camp, being high on the British government's list of subversives. While there he married Muriel Murphy of the family that brewed Murphy's stout. Released in June 1917 he returned to Cork and was re-arrested for wearing a Volunteer uniform, but after three days on hunger strike he was released. One gets the impression that he was almost goading the authorities into action, impatient for a confrontation.

In the immediate post-war general election, in which Sinn Féin routed the old constitutional

Irish Party, he was elected, unopposed, for Mid Cork. On 12 August 1920, by then lord mayor of what had become known as the 'rebel city', he was arrested once again. The charge was possession of seditious papers and a British army cipher. He was tried by court martial four days later and sentenced to two years' imprisonment in Brixton. He went on immediate hunger strike but his physical condition was such that the prison doctor advised against force-feeding. Sixty-nine days later he fell into a coma and five days after that, on 25 October 1920, he died.

His death, even more than MacCurtáin's, shocked the world and caused public opinion in many countries to turn against Britain. Boycotts were threatened and appeals made to the pope. It was to be expected that Germany would be very critical, but when France was equally disturbed even the most right-wing British politicians had to take notice. The two men's deaths undoubtedly helped right-thinking people in America – and Britain – to agitate for the truce which came into effect the following July.

It was clear that Terence was always prepared to make the ultimate sacrifice, as the 1916 leaders had so heroically done. In his play *The Revolutionist* he wrote, as a stage direction, about a patriotic death:

> The last struggle forced the blood to his face; it has not entirely receded and leaves a colour behind with an effect strangely natural. The lines of pain are smoothed out; his expression is strange and happy with the trace of a smile.

Among his final words were: 'I am confident that my death will do more to smash the British empire than my release' and, said to the ministering priest, 'I want you to bear witness that I die a soldier of the Irish Republic.'

MacSwiney's body lay in state for a day in Southwark cathedral but Sinn Féin's plan to bring the body to Dublin was foiled when the authorities commandeered it at Holyhead and had it taken by boat to Cork. He was buried near MacCurtáin in the republican plot at St Finbarr's Cemetery on 31 October 1920, after a huge funeral.

Mary MacSwiney, Terence's sister, took his seat in Dáil Éireann and spoke vigorously against the Treaty in January 1922.

CONSTANCE MARKIEVICZ
&
EVA GORE-BOOTH

Revolutionary, 1868–1927
and Poet, 1870–1926

CONSTANCE GEORGINA GORE-BOOTH was born on 4 February 1868 at Buckingham Gate in London, the elder daughter of Sir Henry (1843–1900) and Lady Georgina. She was two years older than her equally beautiful sister, Eva Selina Laura, born on 22 May 1870.

Sir Henry, who had extensive property at Lissadell, County Sligo, had been an Arctic explorer and was a liberal landlord who took his duties to his tenants seriously, supporting them during the famine of 1879–80. Both of his girls were conscious of the poverty in Ireland and aware of the suffering their parents helped to allay. An early photograph shows the sisters dressed as milkmaids and wearing the metal armbands of the Drumcliffe Cooperative Society, set up by their brother, Josslyn, in 1895.

At nineteen Constance was presented to the queen and was known in London society as the 'new Irish beauty'. Yeats, who was very pleased to be invited to Lissadell, remembered the sisters as 'both beautiful, one a gazelle'. He admired Eva but admitted that Constance bore a striking resemblance to Maud Gonne. Yeats recalled that the father talked of nothing but the North Pole, and he did not think much of Josslyn, the son and heir.

The girls were educated at home in Sligo, where Constance became a fine horsewoman and good shot – convenient for her later career. She intended to become an artist and in 1893 enrolled in the Slade School in London, later moving to the Académie Julian in Paris. There, in 1898 she met the Polish-Ukrainian Count Casimir Dunin Markievicz. Casimir's wife died a year later, and he and Constance married in 1901, returning to Dublin in 1903. They had one child, Maeve, who was born soon after the marriage and was reared by her grandparents at Lissadell. She was eventually estranged from her mother, who was caught up in the artistic life of the capital, producing some impressive landscapes that are on display in the National Gallery in Merrion Square. Although Constance had helped her younger sister, who had become involved in the suffragist movement, to set up a suffrage society in Sligo before Eva left for London, she showed little sign of political involvement at that time.

Eva, who was strongly feminist, had contracted tuberculosis in 1895 and spent some time convalescing in Italy at the villa of George MacDonald, famous for his writings for children. While there she met and fell in love with Esther Roper, the daughter of a Manchester factory hand who later became a missionary in Africa. Esther was involved in the Women's Suffrage movement. They lived together in Manchester until Eva's death on 30 June 1926, and worked for the improvement of the condition of women workers in the textile mills in the city and also for the cause of votes for women. Unlike the Pankhursts, they were strongly pacifist in their agitation and were subject to much abuse for their protests against the Great War. Eva was a talented writer and a confident platform speaker, producing many propaganda leaflets and editing

Women's Labour News. Esther edited her collected poems in 1929 and she is still remembered for the much anthologised 'The Little Waves of Breffny' and 'The Weaver'. Esther nursed her through a prolonged struggle with terminal bowel cancer.

Constance's involvement with republican activism began when, at various 'at-homes' in Dublin, she met Michael Davitt, John O'Leary and Maud Gonne, of whose Inghinidhe na hÉireann ('the daughters of Ireland') she became an active member. She also performed in some of the early Abbey plays. The Abbey was founded by Yeats and Lady Gregory, to 'bring upon the stage the deeper emotions of Ireland'.

In 1908 Constance, actively aided by Eva and Esther, campaigned for the Conservative candidate, William Joynson-Hicks, in the Manchester by-election, because of the Liberal government's proposed licensing bill which would effectively prevent women from being employed in the bar trade. Joynson-Hicks won the election, defeating the Liberal candidate, Winston Churchill.

By then, Constance was thoroughly politicised and the following year, with Bulmer Hobson, she set up the Fianna Éireann, essentially a paramilitary organisation for teenage boys, whom she taught to use firearms. Patrick Pearse later claimed that this was as important to the cause as the foundation of the Irish Volunteers in 1913. She was arrested in 1911 for speaking at a mass meeting organised by the Irish Republican Brotherhood to protest against the visit of the newly crowned George V. Membership of James Connolly's Irish Citizen Army (ICA), the group established for the protection of the locked-out workers during the 1913 strike, followed. She organised soup kitchens at the ICA's headquarters, Liberty Hall, providing money for the food out of her own pocket and eventually having to sell her jewellery for funds.

When Constance agreed to join the ICA, she was given the rank of lieutenant and designed the rather romantic uniform worn by the members who could afford it. During the 1916 Rising, the ICA were stationed in St Stephen's Green, but the trenches they dug in the Green were raked by British fire from the Shelbourne Hotel and they found it advisable to retreat to the more defendable Royal College of Surgeons. Constance was second-in-command to Michael Mallin, and they held out until Sunday 30 April, only surrendering they saw a copy of the order signed by Patrick Pearse. Captain Wheeler, who took the ICA surrender at Surgeons, was a relative of the 'rebel countess'.

Constance was court-martialled in Richmond Barracks, where she stated, 'I did what was right and I stand by it.' Initially condemned to death, her sentence was commuted to life imprisonment by General Sir John Maxwell. He realised too late what a propaganda victory his executions had given the Volunteers and it was feared the execution of a woman would provide even more ammunition for opponents of British policy in Ireland. She was incarcerated in Kilmainham, Mountjoy and later Aylesbury Prison in England.

Released from prison under the general amnesty in 1917, she continued with her struggle for Irish freedom. She was the first woman elected to the House of Commons, in the election held in December 1918, but, like the other Sinn Féin candidates, refused to take her seat in Westminster.

By now a Catholic, she was twice imprisoned during the War of Independence. She was a member of the cabinet of Dáil Éireann (as minister for labour), the first woman to hold such a position; no further women were appointed to cabinet until 1979. Like many other women involved in the politics of the time, she opposed the

Treaty and was active during the Civil War, going on hunger strike when she was arrested again.

In 1926 she presided at Éamon de Valera's launch of Fianna Fáil in the La Scala cinema in Dublin. In the general election in June of the following year she was returned as a Fianna Fáil deputy, but died five weeks later on 15 July 1927, before she could take her seat. Her health had been in decline for some years and she had been badly affected by Eva's death the previous year. While in hospital having an operation on her appendix she developed peritonitis, which proved fatal. At her funeral the ordinary citizens of Dublin lined the streets and supplied eight lorry-loads of flowers that followed her coffin. She was buried in Glasnevin cemetery and is remembered by a sculpture in Rathcormac, County Sligo.

HENRY JOY
&
MARY ANN
McCRACKEN

United Irishman 1767–1798
and Social Reformer 1770–1866

HENRY JOY McCRACKEN was born in High Street, Belfast, essentially the chief thoroughfare of the compact town, on 31 August 1767, and his sister, Mary Ann, three years later on 8 July 1770. The town in which they were born had, during the previous century, gathered a strong reputation for independence and radical beliefs, its citizens mainly Presbyterian. The 'Joy' part of the name came from their maternal grandfather, Francis Joy, who founded Ireland's oldest existing newspaper, the *Belfast News-Letter* in 1737.

The family was of Huguenot descent, and they were prosperous cotton manufacturers. The children were educated 'without the discipline of the rod' at the co-educational school set up in 1755 by David Manson in Clugston's Entry off High Street. Mary showed a talent for mathematics, unlike Henry, who was apprenticed to the linen trade but was too much of a dreamer to apply himself. His maternal relatives, rather unwisely, made him manager of the cotton mill of Holmes and McCracken on the Falls Road. Mary, much more practical, set up a muslin business with her sister, Marjorie. She also involved herself in worthy causes and was instrumental in persuading their young lodger, Edward Bunting, a musical genius, to copy down the traditional tunes played by the competitors at the Belfast Harp Festival in July 1792. (It was also attended by an unimpressed Wolfe Tone, who was heard to mutter, 'Strum, strum, strum and be damned!')

Henry, aflame with the revolutionary fervour that was sweeping in from France since the fall of the Bastille, was attracted to the Society of United Irishmen that had been formed by Tone, Thomas Russell and others in 1791. He became a member of the tenth chapter of the society in March 1795. His position as virtual factory owner, though the business was already failing, gave him the cover he needed to travel about the country recruiting for the revolutionary society. He found willing members among the Defenders (a Catholic agrarian society), though the majority of Ulster members of the United Irishmen were Presbyterian. In June of that year he stood on McArt's Fort, the highest point of Cave Hill overlooking Belfast, in the company of Tone, Russell and Samuel Neilson and swore with them 'never to desist in our efforts until we have subverted the authority of England over our country and asserted our independence'.

Ulster at the time was effectively a police state, with the yeomanry and militias given virtually carte blanche in 'putting down subversion'. Henry was arrested and imprisoned without trial for thirteen months in the newly opened 'Kilmainham Bastille', as he called it in a letter to Mary Ann. He was released on bail on 8 December 1797 after he fell seriously ill, and returned home to Belfast to continue the round of planning, recruiting and attending meetings.

As one of the Ulster delegates to the meeting of the Dublin executive which decided to attempt a rising in May 1798, he was appointed commander-in-chief of Antrim. All was ready by the end of the month and the Ulstermen waited for a signal from Dublin that never came. The system of informers and police spies was so efficient that all the likely revolutionaries there were arrested. On 6 June 1798, tired of waiting, Henry led a small body of men against Antrim town. Their initial success was soon dispelled by the arrival of a large force commanded by General Nugent. Escaping to Colin Glen and Bowhill, north of Belfast, Henry waited while Mary Ann tried to arrange passage for him on a ship to America. He was captured by the Carrickfergus yeomanry on 8 July and brought to Belfast, where, refusing to name his comrades, he was hanged in the Cornmarket nine days later. The resourceful Mary Ann had a surgeon standing by when he was cut down from the scaffold but, after five hours of manipulation, there was no sign of life. He was buried in Antrim, but more than 100 years later Francis Joseph Bigger, the Belfast antiquary, had the remains exhumed and buried beside those of Mary Ann in Clifton Street churchyard.

Mary Ann was twenty-eight when her beloved brother died and she had sixty-eight years
of life ahead of her, which she filled with practical
good works. Her support of the remaining United
Irishmen, especially Thomas Russell, continued,
despite the personal danger. She had probably
fallen in love with Russell and her last letter to
him was typical of her plain speaking and prac-
ticality. She had already adopted Maria, Henry's
illegitimate daughter, and wanted to know if
Russell too, had dependants. She asked, 'if there
are any others who have claims on your affection,
that you will not through motives of false delicacy
scruple to mention them'.

Her most outstanding work was for the Belfast
poor, especially women and children. The muslin
business finally failed in 1815 but while it lasted
she maintained the highest standards of worker
care, as befitted an active campaigner against
slavery and, as a follower of Elizabeth Fry, prison

reformer. She was very specific about the principles that should govern employment: 'Workers … ought to be provided with warm coats and cloaths [*sic*] so as to be protected against the evil effects of wet and cold … Sufficient time should be allowed for amusement in the open air … A very serious responsibility attaches to those who employ children.' She was particularly incensed by the barbaric practice of having young boys climb up chimneys to sweep them.

In old age she was one of the best sources for R. R. Madden's seven-volume *The United Irishmen: Their Lives and Times* (1842–46), carrying on a regular correspondence with him in her seventies. Her last years were spent in a house in Donegall Pass in Belfast, where she died on 26 July 1866, eighteen days after her ninety-sixth birthday. A Wedgwood blue plate, affixed to the house by the Ulster History Circle, matches one in High Street that marks a location near Henry's birthplace.

NANO NAGLE

Founder of Presentation Order
1718–1784

HONORIA 'NANO' NAGLE was born at
Ballygriffin in the beautiful valley of the
River Blackwater, near Mallow, County Cork, in
1718, the daughter of Garret Nagle. Nagle was a
rarity at that time – a rich Catholic. The family
had been minor aristocrats associated with the
overthrown Stuart dynasty but had managed to
retain their land and their wealth. Her mother,
Ann Mathews, was of an equally prosperous old
family from County Tipperary.

The strict application at that time of the
Popery Laws was largely successful in making
native Irish Catholics an under-class, by depriv-
ing them of the ability to own or buy land, hold

office or have their children educated. Bishops were, at least in theory, exiled, and priests were to show no evidence of their sacred office and be referred to as Mr Brown or Mr Murphy. Younger sons were sent abroad to join European armies and engage in military activities 'from Tobruk to Belgrade'. Daughters, felt to be more appropriate for education, were sent to France, though it was an offence by law to arrange this. Edmund Burke, a relative of Nano's on her mother's side, later summarised the penal enactments as follows: 'Their declared object was to reduce the Catholics in Ireland to a miserable populace without property, without estimation, without education.'

Nano, as she was universally known, initially attended the local hedge school. For further education, a trip to France was necessary, and this was arranged through the Nagles of Cork, kinsmen and rich merchants. Nano and her sister,

Ann, were smuggled in the merchant ships that brought continental wines to Ireland and returned with Irish meat and whiskey. They received a fashionable education and happily enjoyed the social life of the French capital in the gaudy reign of the pleasure-loving Louis XV. However, in spite of the gaiety, they could not but be conscious of the terrible poverty that co-existed with the frivolous aristocracy of the *Ancien Régime*.

The sisters returned to Ireland on the death of their father and lived for a time with their mother in Dublin, where the poverty of the people was even greater and more obvious than in Paris. Ann once sold a valuable piece of silk to relieve a distressed family and hearing of this, Nano began to consider how she too might do something to relieve the misery of the Irish poor.

At first, she tried an approved but oblique method, becoming a religious sister so that she might pray for them effectively. She entered an

Ursuline convent in Paris but was eventually persuaded by the convent chaplain that her true vocation was at home, helping educate the children who were totally deprived of any means of improvement. In 1749,
when she was thirty-one, she left the convent and returned to Cork, where her brother Joseph lived. She rented a shack in Cove Lane, in defiance of the law and without the knowledge of her brother. She gathered about thirty children into the Cove Lane school and began the first rudimentary education the poor in Cork had known.

The school prospered and within a year 200 children were receiving a free education. By 1757 she had opened five schools for girls and two for boys. She organised teachers and ran the schools by day, while at night, with no sense of fear, she visited the poverty-stricken sick and elderly carrying a single light that gained her the nickname 'The Lady with the Lantern' seventy years before Florence Nightingale was born.

In 1771, troubled by ill-health, she invited the French Ursulines with whom she had lived, to come to teach the children but, as they were an enclosed order and used to teaching the children of the rich, she found them unsuitable. Having an instinctive inclination to the religious life, in 1775 she and some willing followers entered a novitiate in her newly established religious order, the 'Sisters of the Charitable Instruction of the Sacred Heart of Jesus'. The following year, in June, these women took the veil and Nano took the name Mother Mary of St John of God, after the Portuguese patron of nurses. The name of the order was later changed to 'Sisters of the

Presentation of the Blessed Virgin' (SPBV) and the lantern became its symbol.

By the time of Nano's death, on 26 April 1784, there were 400 pupils being educated in a network of schools throughout Cork. Nano financed these with the considerable wealth left to her by members of her family and, when that was gone, by begging; she was often taken for a pauper in the streets. In 1782 Luke Gardiner's Catholic Relief Act allowed the Nagle schools to come out of the shadows and continue their work. It was, of course, a religious education but the Three Rs (reading, 'riting and 'rithmetic) were not neglected.

Nano's religious life was intense; it was only when her body was being prepared for burial that it was discovered that her knees had been in a state of ulceration for many years. Her father once said, 'Poor Nano will yet be a saint' and the process for having her declared such is well advanced, with Pope Francis declaring her 'Venerable' in 2013. She set an example that would be followed in the next century by Mary Aikenhead with her Sisters of Charity, and Catherine McAuley with the Sisters of Mercy. The extremely slow reform of conditions in Ireland meant that their work was also necessary.

One event that Nano might not have approved of was the formal papal approval given by Pope Pius VII to the SPBV in 1802. He imposed strict enclosure on the order and confined their activities to teaching. Face-to-face engagement with the very poor was no longer allowed, and it was left to the later sisterhoods of Aikenhead and McAuley to continue that aspect of Nano's work.

DANIEL O'CONNELL

The Liberator
1775–1847

DANIEL O'CONNELL was born on 6 August 1775 in Carhan, near Caherciveen, in the Iveragh peninsula of west Kerry. His father, Morgan, was one of twenty-two children and though not prosperous, managed to subsist as a grazier, merchant and, most significantly, a smuggler. In this he was supported by his much richer brother, Maurice, known universally as 'Hunting Cap', who did what he could to care for his many tenants-at-will. In keeping with an age-old custom, the young O'Connell was fostered with this rich, childless relative at Derrynane House, near Caherdaniel.

In 1791 Daniel and his brother Maurice were

sent to school in France. Their sojourn there was short. Their arrival coincided with the worst excesses of the Revolution and they were advised to head for England in January 1793, the same month that saw the guillotining of Louis XVI and his family. The experience of that journey, harassed by unthinking mobs, left O'Connell terrified, and he later refused to countenance violence as a means of achieving political ends, an attitude that became his greatest strength as well as the cause of his final eclipse.

His qualifications in law, just then permitted to Catholics, were obtained in Lincoln's Inns in 1794 in London, and at King's Inns on Constitution Hill in Dublin in 1796. When the United Irishmen began their short rebellion in 1798, he joined the Lawyers Artillery Corps of yeomanry. For the next decade he worked on the Munster circuit, becoming one of the finest and cleverest advocates the country had ever seen.

He was the supreme actor as barrister, mocking and impersonating, switching from declamation to cheap comedy. His physical strength was awesome but necessary, as he travelled to hearings in Roscrea, Nenagh, Limerick, Ennis, Macroom, Cork and Cashel at least twice a year, over appalling roads and dangerous mountain passes. O'Connell had to subsist on low fees since he was barred from the rank of senior counsel because of his religion – and though he could vote he could not become a member of the House of Commons.

His witty tongue frequently got him into trouble. Calling Sir Robert Peel 'Orange' Peel was perhaps inevitable, since the chief secretary was no friend of Catholics. It is also said that O'Connell claimed Peel's smile was like the sunbeam on a coffin plate, so it is no wonder that they became sworn enemies, which was a pity since Peel was not the worst of Ireland's rulers.

In his twenty-sixth year he met his third cousin, Mary O'Connell, in Tralee, when he was appearing in the North Kerry assizes. With customary urgency he asked, 'Will you engage yourself to me?' She agreed and was happy to keep their affair secret, for fear of offending Hunting Cap. Tired of waiting for a suitable time to tell his guardian, on an impulse he persuaded the parish priest of Tralee to officiate at a secret ceremony on 24 July 1802. Mary soon became pregnant and Hunting Cap, with typical fury, changed his will so that his ward received only one-third of his estate. He did, however, leave Derrynane to his nephew, which became a reliable place of rest and refreshment for him, and is now a fascinating O'Connell Museum. Of Daniel and Mary's many children, three daughters and four sons survived into adulthood. But as he eventually reached the stature of a mythic figure, Daniel was inevitably credited with multiple children throughout Munster.

The Act of Union (1801) that deprived Ireland of its own limited parliament, gave O'Connell the impetus to enter politics. He felt it was his destiny to repeal the act, and for this he had to become a member of the Westminster parliament. Because the law kept Catholics from becoming MPs, his first crusade was to have this law revoked and make sure that his people were properly represented.

In 1811 he formed the Catholic Board and in 1823 the wider Catholic Association. These were funded by the simple expedient of having each household pay a penny per month, a levy that most could afford and one that brought in a large fighting fund. Some of the money was used to compensate voters who, in the days before the Ballot Act of 1872 (which allows voters to cast their vote in secret), were at the mercy of their landlords if they did not support the candidate he backed. O'Connell himself stood for Clare in the general election of 1828, despite being ineligible to sit in parliament, and easily defeated the pro-government candidate. Wellington and Peel, prime minister and home secretary respectively, alarmed at the consequences of denying Catholic emancipation were finally able to persuade George IV that it must be granted. It was O'Connell's finest hour.

Once emancipation was granted in 1829, all of his energies as the undoubted leader of the Irish people, the 'King of the Beggars' as Frank O'Connor called him, went into his crusade for the repeal of the Act of Union. In a sense, he created modern Ireland and though he failed to achieve the goal of repeal, he started the process that others followed. From early in the 1840s he had the support of the middle-class movement known as Young Ireland. Thirty-one mass meetings held in 1843 in centres such as Limerick, Kells, Charleville, Cork, Cashel and Mullaghmast culminated in a 'monster' meeting at Tara that attracted an estimated 750,000 people to hear his vocally unassisted oratory on 15 August. The climax of Repeal Year was to be a meeting at Clontarf on Sunday 8 October but, true to his pacifist stance, when Peel proscribed the meeting O'Connell acquiesced and cancelled it. Despite this he was charged with sedition and in 1844 was sentenced to a year's imprisonment in the Richmond Bridewell and fined £2,000. The cancellation also cost him the support of the Young Irelanders. After three months in prison, O'Connell was released and brought home in a beautifully decorated open coach.

Already ill with the cerebral abscess that would lead to meningitis and kill him, weary with the struggles over the future of education, and horrified at the effects of the Great Famine, O'Connell set out for Rome at the beginning of March 1847. He reached Genoa by painful stages in poor physical condition – he had never fully recovered from a savage surgery for the removal of piles in 1842 – and he died there two days after arriving. On his instructions, his heart was placed in a shrine and deposited in the Irish College in Rome, while his body was taken home to Ireland to be buried in Glasnevin, thus fulfilling the mantra learned by many generations of Irish schoolchildren: 'My soul to heaven, my heart to Rome and my body to Ireland.'

JEREMIAH
O'DONOVAN ROSSA

Revolutionary
1831–1915

JEREMIAH DONOVAN (the O' and the Rossa were added later, the latter a tribute to the headlands of his beloved south-west Cork) was born in Rosscarbery, County Cork in September 1831, the son of Ellen O'Driscoll and Denis Donovan, a tenant farmer. During the worst years of the famine, though still in his teens, he helped distribute food to the starving and saw his own father perish and his family emigrate. Jeremiah moved twelve miles to Skibbereen, a town that suffered greatly during the 'Hungry Forties'.

As a result of his experiences during the Great

Famine, he became a confirmed nationalist and in 1856 he gathered a number of like-minded individuals round him to form the Phoenix National and Literary Society, which had the stated aim of 'the liberation of Ireland by force of arms'. Fed by nationalist newspaper *The Nation* and the reputation of the men of Young Ireland, he was prepared to wait until there was some hope of a united front against the common enemy. Though independent and geographically remote in west Cork, when the Phoenix members heard the news of the foundation of the Irish Revolutionary Brotherhood (IRB; the Revolutionary soon changed to Republican) by James Stephens on St Patrick's Day 1858, associate membership, if not actual amalgamation, seemed desirable.

The use of the word 'phoenix', with its connotation of new life rising out of the ashes, made it clear to Stephens that O'Donovan Rossa and his Phoenix Society should be encouraged, and they quickly became 'Fenians', a common name for the new nationalist group. However, the brotherhood had little cohesion, despite the fact that it straddled the Atlantic, with a sister organisation, the Fenian Brotherhood, based in America. In Ireland it consisted of a number of small 'circles' in various cities with little to connect them except general Fenian membership and a grave suspicion of the capabilities of the titular head, Stephens. In spite of elaborate security, government spies soon informed the authorities about the new subversive, and hardly secret, society. In a swoop by the RIC in December 1858, all known IRB members, including O'Donovan Rossa, were arrested on suspicion of the offence of treason and imprisoned without trial. They were released the following July for lack of evidence. The American group was anxious for action but there had been no law-breaking except the administering of oaths. The Phoenix flame was still tamped down and its flaming was further postponed with the outbreak of the American Civil War (1861–65).

In 1863 Stephens founded the *Irish People* newspaper to represent the cause and since O'Donovan Rossa was a trader with a literary bent, he was the obvious person to be appointed business manager. But the government spies who had infiltrated the IRB even had spies on the staff of the *Irish People*. On 15 September 1865 the police arrested all known Fenians on its staff, including Thomas Clarke Luby, John O'Leary and O'Donovan Rossa. Stephens and Charles Kickham were arrested two months later, although Stephens escaped on 24 November with the help of two Fenian warders.

O'Donovan Rossa was not so lucky. Tried at the Green Street Courthouse, he seemed to go out of his way to annoy the presiding judge, Judge Keogh. He insisted on being given time to read all the documents relevant to his prosecution, including copies of the newspapers in which his and the judge's name figured, complaining that for that reason the trial should not be allowed to proceed. His complaint was ignored and he was sentenced to penal servitude for life. His sentence was served in the English jails of Pentonville, Portland, Millbank and Chatham, where he endured cruel and unnatural punishments that included cell isolation with his hands manacled behind his back. He left a stark account of those years in his *Prison Life* (1874).

The severity of the sentence reflected his record as a persistent member of the IRB.

In 1869 O'Donovan Rossa was elected to the House of Commons as member for Tipperary, despite still being incarcerated. The election was declared invalid because he was a convicted felon, but the British government was susceptible to this demonstration of Irish public opinion and a Fenian amnesty was declared in 1870. O'Donovan Rossa was released from jail on condition that he go into permanent exile from Ireland. It must have been with some relief that he boarded the SS *Cuba* en route for New York in January 1871.

Once in America, he resumed his Fenian activities. He openly advocated the dynamiting campaign carried out by Fenians in major British cities from 1881 to 1885. His extradition to Ireland was demanded several times from Congress because of his continuing collection of money for what he called the 'Skirmishing Fund', intended to help nationalists free Ireland from British rule. This was possibly the reason for his shooting in 1885, outside his Broadway office, by Yseult Dudley, an Englishwoman who many claimed was in the pay of some branch of the British secret service, though the government denied this.

His exile was not absolute; O'Donovan Rossa visited his homeland in 1894 and again in 1904 when he was made a freeman of Cork. By then he was mainly retired and at odds with the members of Clan na Gael, the Irish-American group that succeeded the Fenian Brotherhood and advocated waiting for England's difficulty and, therefore, Ireland's opportunity.

O'Donovan Rossa was married three times and had eighteen children. In 1853 he married Nora (Nanno) Eager of Skibbereen; in 1861 Eileen Buckley of Castlehaven, who died in

1863; and in 1864 Molly Irwin of Clonakilty, by whom he had thirteen of his children.

He died on 29 June 1915 at St Vincent's Hospital, Staten Island, and when the news reached Ireland, Thomas Clarke, himself a former member of Clan na Gael and a member of the IRB and Irish Volunteers, organised for the body to be brought home for a hero's burial. On 1 August 1915, in front of a huge crowd, Patrick Pearse made his famous prophetic speech: 'The fools, the fools – they have left us our Fenian dead, and while Ireland holds these graves, Ireland unfree shall never be at peace.'

CHARLES STEWART PARNELL

Political Leader
1846–1892

CHARLES STEWART PARNELL was born on 27 June 1846 at Avondale, County Wicklow, the country estate of his father, John Henry. His mother, Delia, was American, the daughter of a naval hero of the War of 1812 against the British, and his grandfather had suggested the device of the 'penny rent' to O'Connell as a means of financing his political campaigns. The atmosphere in the house was tempered by liberal thought. Two of his sisters, Fanny (1848–1882) and Anna (1852–1911), were also cognisant of the need for reform of the political and landholding situation in Ireland.

Parnell received a traditional education in several schools in England. After the death of his father, Parnell inherited the Avondale estate in 1859 and he became lord of Avondale on his twenty-first birthday, proving to be a benevolent if economically unsound landlord. Following school he attended Magdalene College in Cambridge, but left in 1869 without taking a degree, having been suspended for a minor offence and financial trouble.

Conscious of the turmoil in the aftermath of the Fenian rising of 1867, he decided to take the family view of contemporary politics, presenting himself at the office of the admired Isaac Butt, who had founded a movement for Home Rule. Butt was delighted with the new recruit, not realising that Parnell was to be his nemesis. Parnell had few of Butt's capabilities, learning, rhetorical skills or charm, but he schooled himself to overcome these inadequacies.

In 1875 Parnell was elected MP for Meath as part of the Irish Parliamentary Party formed in 1874 by Butt. Once in parliament, he developed the technique of obstructionism begun by the abrasive member for Cavan, the Belfast butcher Joseph Biggar, in order to prevent bills on Ireland being passed.

In 1879 Butt retired, badly upstaged by the unemotional and essentially unreadable Parnell, who became the head of the Home Rule movement. Parnell seemed, chameleon-like, to take on the colour of his surrounding and make appropriate noises. His contribution to the Land War of the 1870s and 1880s was exemplified in his speech in Ennis on 19 September 1880, in which he advised the 'boycotting' of any person who took an evicted tenant's holding 'by leaving him severely alone, by putting him into a sort of moral Coventry, by isolating him from the rest of his kind as if he were a leper of old …' The word was taken from 'Captain' Charles Boycott, whose workforce was warned off his lands in County Mayo after some tenants on his estate were served with eviction notices.

The technique and the work of Land Leaguers effectively won the Land War, while the slightly opportunistic Parnell concentrated his efforts and that of his party on achieving some form of Home Rule. William Ewart Gladstone, the slightly unctuous voice of British liberalism, made a kind of uneasy alliance with the man who, after a triumphant and lucrative tour of America, was elected for three constituencies in the election of 1880. It was his finest hour, leading his future adversary Tim Healy to dub him the 'uncrowned king of Ireland'.

It was also in 1880 that Parnell met Katharine O'Shea (1845–1921), the English wife of Captain William O'Shea, and they became lovers. On 13 October 1881 Parnell and other leaders of the

Land League were arrested and imprisoned in Kilmainham Gaol because of their attacks on the Land Act, which they felt did not offer enough rights to the tenants.

Now it was the turn of Parnell's sisters to carry on the fight. Fanny Parnell had lived in New Jersey since 1874 and, as a popular poet, was able to keep the cause of the Irish tenantry before the sympathetic American public. Her poem 'After Death' is in many anthologies and Davitt described 'Hold the Harvest' as the '*Marseillaise* of the Irish peasant'. Her agitation ceased when she died suddenly of heart failure in July 1882.

Back in Ireland Anna Parnell swung into action immediately after her brother's arrest, founding the Ladies' Land League to carry on the work of withholding rent, boycotting and resisting evictions. Her women distributed prefabricated wooden huts to shelter the dispossessed. Anna's commitment to the cause was much more overt than that of her brother and they parted on bad terms when, even though £60,000 (about €4.3 million today) in relief was distributed, he disbanded her League. Her book, *Tale of a Great Sham*, published posthumously, was severely critical of the men's handling of the struggle. She went to live in England and changed her name. She drowned at Ilfracombe in Devon in 1911.

Parnell's not terribly burdensome imprisonment lasted seven months until, under the terms of the so-called Kilmainham Treaty, he and the others were released and Gladstone introduced the first of a series of land acts that eventually settled the land question.

The murder of the liberal Lord Frederick

Cavendish in Phoenix Park, Dublin, in 1882 by an extreme group of the IRB calling themselves the 'Invincibles', was a blow to Parnell but Gladstone persuaded him not to resign. It might have been better for him if he had, but he was sure that he could win Home Rule, forgetting the shared intransigence of Ulster's unionists and the House of Lords. There was also his affair with Katharine. Although things seemed to go well at first and Captain O'Shea seemed satisfied with a safe parliamentary seat in Clare, relations soured and he threatened to name Parnell in a divorce case. He could have been bought off with £20,000 but he had already taken all of Katharine's savings and the couple could not pay.

When O'Shea filed for divorce and named Parnell as co-respondent it was a grievous blow to the couple, the party and Gladstone, who needed the support of MPs who were 'chapel' and publicly censorious. Moreover, the Catholic

Church had been the most effective and widespread support system Parnell had. The timing was especially galling, as Parnell's stock had never been higher. Just a few months earlier, it was proved that letters supposedly written by him advocating violence, and printed by *The Times* in 1887, were forgeries.

The decree nisi was granted on 17 November 1891 and, at an extremely private ceremony in a registry office in Steyning, near Brighton, on 25 June 1892 Parnell and his 'Queenie' were married. By 6 October he was dead – his marriage lasted just 104 days.

The last year of his life was spent in brazening out the effect his private life was having, trying to hold on to political power and rallying what supporters he could to his side. He was clearly ill but adamant that he would fight to retain his position. It proved too much for a body he had remorselessly punished.

Parnell's refusal to resign from the Irish Parliamentary Party after he was named in the divorce case led to a split that rendered the party, once so strong and efficient, weak and ineffective. It took all the patience and skill of his disciple John Redmond to bind up wounds and reorganise the party. He was so successful in this that Home Rule was almost within reach when the Great War broke out in August 1914.

Parnell was buried after a great public funeral in Glasnevin. His grave is marked by a simple granite boulder with the word Parnell carved upon it, and it lies close to the soaring round tower that marks Daniel O'Connell's last resting place. It is fitting that two of Ireland's greatest leaders should be together.

Katharine lived until 1921 and is buried in Littlehampton Cemetery in Sussex, England.

PATRICK H. PEARSE

Poet, Educationalist, Revolutionary
1879–1916

PATRICK HENRY PEARSE was born on 10 November 1879, the son of an Englishman, James Pearse (1839–1900), who came to work in Dublin as a monumental sculptor, and Margaret Brady his second wife. Although Patrick would often use an Irish form of his name, Pádraig Mac Piarais, on the Proclamation of Independence that he read on the steps of the General Post Office (GPO) on Easter Monday his name is given as P. H. Pearse. He had two sisters, one older and one younger, and a brother, Willie, born on 15 November 1881 and essentially his closest friend.

The brothers were educated at the Irish Christian Brothers school in Westland Row, just round the corner from 27 Great Brunswick Street (now Pearse Street) where he was born. Pearse was enamoured of the whole panoply of Irish history and heritage, from mythical times to the contemporary campaign for Home Rule, which by the first decade of the twentieth century seemed more than just a vague possibility. He was a quiet young man, conscious of a slight cast in one eye, so many of his photographs were posed in profile. He enrolled in the Royal University of Ireland (RUI) in 1898 and in King's Inns that same year. By June 1901 he had graduated from the RUI with a second-class honours BA in Irish, English and French. He was called to the Bar in the same year but, apart from one case in 1905 about the labelling of a cart in Irish, for which he was briefed by the Gaelic League, he had no further dealings with the courts. (This incident gave rise to the popular satirical song *An Trucailín Donn*, 'The Little Brown Cart').

Pearse had joined the Gaelic League in 1896 when it was barely three years old and, though he found some of its stalwarts extremely narrow and chauvinistic in their attitudes, accepted the editorship of *An Claidheamh Soluis* ('The Sword of Light'), the league's chief organ and sturdier successor to *Fáinne an Lae* ('Dawn'), in 1903. It took its name from the invincible sword of Nuada, the chief of the Tuatha Dé Danann.

On 1 November 1913 'The North Began', Eoin MacNeill's article on the formation of the Ulster Volunteer Force, their importation of arms and his idea of forming an equivalent nationalist organisation, was published in *An Claidheamh Soluis*. MacNeill's ideas changed Pearse from a middle-class constitutional supporter of John Redmond into, in his own words, 'the most dangerous revolutionary of them all'. Convinced by MacNeill's account of the unyielding determination of Ulster Unionists, he helped launch the Irish Volunteers three weeks after the publication of the article. Until then Pearse had seemed to his colleagues a poet, a dreamer, a schoolmaster, but, on the recommendation of Thomas Clarke, he was soon made a member of the Irish Republican Brotherhood (IRB) and by 1915 he was a member of its Supreme Council.

Though a brilliant pamphleteer, Pearse was not a good speaker. His most effective piece of rhetorical composition was his address at the burial of Jeremiah O'Donovan Rossa on 1 August 1915 with its triumphant conclusion: 'Ireland unfree will never be at peace', yet on the day his speech was largely inaudible.

At this time the Irish school system educated Irish children to be 'good Englishmen', so in 1908 Pearse had opened a bilingual school called St Enda's (Scoil Éanna), named after a fifth-century teacher of Irish monks, in Dublin. There, each child was helped to develop as an individual, as described in *The Murder Machine* (the name of a series of articles on education he published in 1913). The mythical and historical heroes of the school were Pearse's own heroes, including Cú Chulainn, whose motto became that of the school: 'I care not though I were to live but one day and one night if only my fame and my deeds live after me.' The other heroes as he saw them were Wolfe Tone, Thomas Davis, John Mitchel and James Fintan Lalor.

It is said that when his pupils went home for their Easter holidays in 1916 Pearse bade them farewell with 'benign resignation' as he knew the Rising was to take place and he believed he would not return. In spite of many setbacks, not least the demobilisation call by MacNeill, the Irish Volunteers occupied various strategic buildings around Dublin on 24 April, most famously the GPO in Sackville Street which became the headquarters for the rebellion. The Rising quickly became, in Pearse's words, 'a bloody protest for a glorious thing' and just five days after the reading of the Proclamation of the Irish Republic on the steps of the GPO, he ordered the surrender of the Irish forces.

On 3 May Pearse was executed by firing squad at Arbour Hill Barracks, along with Thomas MacDonagh and Tom Clarke, his revolutionary sponsor. Willie, who had been with his brother in the GPO and had also helped him run St Enda's, was shot the following day.

The signatories of the Proclamation had expected martyrdom. They hoped to rekindle strong fires of nationalism in the Irish people, but initially all they seemed to have stirred was mockery and looting. However, because of the arrogance and brutality of General Sir John Maxwell, who had made himself virtual military dictator of the country, and the inertia of Herbert Asquith, the British prime minister, the sneering populace quickly became patriots when faced with the British reaction to the Rising. Asquith realised too late that Maxwell's policy of executions and widespread arrests had given the Volunteers the victory of which they had dreamed.

Pearse was a poet and a dreamer but, in spite of his social awkwardness and strangeness, he proved to be, in the words of another Irish poet, 'a mover and shaker of the world'.

JENNIE WYSE POWER

Feminist and Senator
1858–1941

JENNIE O'TOOLE was born in May 1858 in Baltinglass, County Wicklow, where her father had a shop on the main street selling leather goods and other provisions. The business failed when she was two years old and the family moved to Dublin. The family had a long-standing nationalist tradition: a Fenian uncle had been out in the 1867 rising and it was not surprising that Jennie became a member of the Ladies' Land League in 1881, acting as a compiler of the 'Book of Kells', the record of all evictions that proved essential to the Plan of Campaign against absentee landlords. She also organised the league in her home county of Wicklow, and in Carlow.

In 1883 she married John Wyse Power, a journalist with *The Freeman's Journal* and a member of the Irish Republican Brotherhood (IRB). Later he joined with Michael Cusack in founding the Gaelic Athletic Association (GAA), an organisation which, if not actually subversive, proved a rich source for the recruiting of subversives. The couple had four children, one of whom, Nancy, played an active part in the Easter Rising as a courier and afterwards became the first woman to rise to the rank of principal officer in the Irish civil service.

Jennie supported Charles Stewart Parnell, even after news broke of his affair with Katharine O'Shea, and published a collection of his speeches in 1892, shortly after his death, called *Words of a Dead Chief.* She joined the Gaelic League soon after its establishment in July 1893 and in 1900 became vice-president of Inghinidhe na hÉireann ('The Daughters of Ireland'), the society founded that year by Maud Gonne that was revolutionary, feminist and worked for the rights of women. Its members understood that feminism implicitly required assistance for the poor. She was one of a number of women who combined patriotism with a strong urge to improve the position of women in Irish society, a consideration far down the list of male nationalist priorities.

Typical of Jennie's character and career was her acceptance of an appointment as a public guardian, responsible for the operation of the Dickensian Poor Law, and equally typical was the fact that she was dismissed from the post eight years later because of her attempts to reform a system that essentially preferred low municipal rates to genuine charity.

In 1905 Arthur Griffith founded Sinn Féin, a movement for self-government that involved no violence but would have meant the inevitable irrelevance of the British involvement in Irish affairs. Jennie served on the executive from its inception and was joint treasurer from 1909. By 1911 she was vice-president, along with Countess Markievicz, and played a leading part in organising the funeral of the old Fenian Jeremiah O'Donovan Rossa on 1 August 1915, at which Pearse's statement, 'The fools! The fools! They have left us our Fenian dead, and while Ireland holds these graves, Ireland unfree shall never be at peace', was a declaration of intent.

In 1915 Jennie, with her usual nonchalance, was made president of the militant Cumann na mBan ('The League of Women'), the auxiliary women's branch of the Irish Volunteers founded in 1914. By then she had a shop and restaurant, famous for its freshly obtained country food, at 21 Henry Street in Dublin. She also lived above the premises, which was used as a convenient meeting place for those planning the 1916 Rising. Seven of the thirteen men executed in May 1916 signed the iconic Proclamation of the Republic there.

Jennie's daughter, Nancy, was one of a number of emissaries sent to provincial commanders to countermand the orders to stand down issued by Eoin MacNeill on Holy Saturday 1916. Despite the fighting, on her return to Dublin Nancy succeeded in making her way to the GPO to report to Pearse.

During Easter Week Jennie supplied the various Volunteer outposts, most conveniently the GPO, with provisions, until her shop was destroyed by British artillery. In the aftermath of the Rising, she and Nancy used their dazzling administrative abilities to tend to the families of the 3,430 men and seventy-nine women who were arrested after the surrender. (Of these, 1,424 men and all but five of the women were released within six weeks.)

Jennie became an executive member of the reconstituted Sinn Féin and was Constance Markievicz's chief election agent in her successful election to Westminster in the post-war general election held in December 1918. She was the Sinn Féin treasurer during the War of Independence, with Nancy acting as her secretary. Nancy, who had been a student at Bonn, was sent to Germany in 1921 to establish an information office about the Irish struggle.

Unlike many of her close allies, Jennie was pro-Treaty and joined Cumann na Saoirse ('The League of Freedom'), the rival to Cumann na mBan which had repudiated the Treaty. She became a trustee of Cumann na nGaedheal ('The Party of the Irish'), which formed the first government of the newly established Saorstát Éireann ('Irish Free State'), and was appointed to the Senate in 1922, one of two women so honoured. She later grew disenchanted with Cumann na nGaedheal's apparent acquiescence in the partition of Ireland and drifted towards her natural home in the newly formed Fianna Fáil party.

Of the two causes for which Jennie battled all her life, republicanism and feminism (including concern for the poor), the latter was dearer to her heart and she continued her campaign for equality for women. She parted company with Fianna Fáil when their Conditions of Employment Bill was seen to discriminate against women. She retired from the senate in 1936 and died on 5 January 1941.

Nancy continued to work within the civil service to do what she could to counteract the blatant discrimination against women there, and died in 1963.

PATRICK SARSFIELD

Jacobite Soldier
c. 1650–1693

PATRICK SARSFIELD, the first Earl of Lucan, took his title from his birthplace, Lucan Castle in County Dublin. Little else is known about his birth and early life, although a possible date of birth is 1650. His father, also Patrick, had married into Irish nobility, taking Anne, the daughter of Rory O'More, one of the organisers of the rising of 1641, as his wife. The family was Catholic, with an estate bringing in £2,000 a year (about €180,000 today).

As befitted a younger son of a good family with no zest for the Church, he was sent to France for training as a soldier and on 6 February 1678 enlisted in Sir Thomas Dougan's regiment of foot with the rank of captain. He achieved distinction at the Battle of Sedgemoor on 6 July 1685, when he helped rout the forces of the Duke of Monmouth, who was attempting to usurp the throne of James II. This was a cause of some anxiety to him since his older brother, William, had married Monmouth's sister, and he himself had served in Monmouth's regiment when the duke's father, Charles II, was on the throne of England. But Patrick's loyalty to James was unyielding and his heroism in charging the opposing force at the head of his men earned him praise and promotion from the king.

In an attempt to undermine Protestant rule in Ireland, James sent Patrick to Ireland with Richard Talbot, Earl of Tyrconnell, who had been made commander-in-chief of the army in Ireland. But when a son was born to James' Catholic second wife in 1688, the English Protestant establishment effectively dethroned him.

James chose Ireland as the base from which he would fight to restore his position. Sarsfield was rapidly promoted to brigadier and then major-general. This last distinction was given with some reluctance since James, who was no fool, reportedly called him 'a brave fellow, but very scantily supplied with brains'.

During the war between William of Orange (often remembered as 'King Billy') and James, Sarsfield helped secure Connacht for James. But when the two kings met on 1 July 1690 at Oldcastle on the Boyne river, James' forces were defeated, largely due to inertia and mis-judgement on the part of the king and Tyrconnell.

James, to his eternal ignominy, fled the field and Sarsfield could do little but retreat with his regiment to Limerick.

General Lauzun, who commanded the French troops that Louis XIV had sent to aid James, and Tyrconnell felt that Limerick could not be held. According to Lauzun, the city walls could not withstand a barricade of rotten apples let alone English and Dutch cannonballs. They moved north of the Shannon to Galway taking most of the heavy artillery and French soldiers with them, and leaving the French General de Boisseleau in charge of Limerick, with Sarsfield in command of the cavalry.

William's forces reached Limerick in early August and besieged the city. However, their initial attacks were largely ineffective. The reason for this became clear to James' army when a French Huguenot deserter explained that William was still waiting for the arrival of his siege train, which brought with it his heavy artillery (six 24-pounder and two 18-pounder cannons), sixty ammunition wagons with 27,000kg of gunpowder and 3,000 cannonballs, and pontoons essential for crossing the river. It also carried three days' rations for the army. The French gunner was able to provide the route of the train on its way from Cashel.

Sarsfield mustered the cavalry and, guided by a local raparee called Daniel Hogan, known as 'Galloping Hogan', intercepted the siege train at Ballyneety, about four miles from Limerick. One of the legends associated with this raid claims that some of Sarsfield's scouts found the wife of a Williamite soldier bathing her feet in a stream and, taking her to an inn at Cullen near Tipperary town, found out that the password at the intended campsite near Ballyneety Castle was to be 'Sarsfield'. The story goes that Sarsfield, when challenged by a sentry at the camp, replied: 'Sarsfield is the word and Sarsfield is the man!'

In an attempt to destroy as much as they could, Sarsfield's men filled the cannons with powder, rammed their muzzles into the ground, piled the wagons on top and laid a trail of gunpowder that they then ignited. Though not all of the arms were put out of action, the raid was sufficient to delay the attack on Limerick and hearten its Jacobite defenders. Sarsfield was made Earl of Lucan by King James.

The siege continued, but a determined attack by William on the city failed and led to severe losses for his army, which, along with the depletion of ammunition and the approach of autumn with its bad weather resulted in the Williamite army withdrawing.

Although William left Ireland, the war between his forces and those of James continued. However, following a disastrous defeat for James' army at Aughrim in July 1691 and the subsequent capitulation of Galway, Limerick once again found itself besieged. Having proved his capability as a tactician, Sarsfield now showed considerable diplomatic skill in negotiation, arranging the city's surrender to the now victorious Williamite army.

The resulting Treaty of Limerick had two elements: military and civil. Sarsfield wished to keep his army intact, with the hope of some future action against the British. He did not realise that the Irish episodes were the least significant part of the 'War of the Three Kings' – James, William and Louis – but he knew that under the terms of the treaty he had some hope of retaining power for the now permanently exiled James. The Irish soldiers, with their wives and children, were to be granted safe passage to France, and this part of the treaty was largely upheld. However, the terms granting Catholics religious freedom and the retention of their lands were soon repudiated by both the Protestant Dublin parliament and the one in London. Sarsfield himself lost his lands and the yearly stipend associated with them, and his soldiers became known as the 'wild geese', who would fight 'on far foreign fields from Tobruk to Belgrade' for many foreign monarchs, usually against Britain.

It was in a war between Louis and William that Sarsfield lost his life, two years later. The Low Countries, as ever the 'cockpit of Europe', were the scene of most of the fighting. At Neerwinden (in modern Belgium) on 19 July 1693, near a stream called Landen, Sarsfield was hit in the chest by a musket ball and he died at Huy on 22 July. As he was stretchered off the field he is said to have pressed his hand over the bloody wound and cried: 'Would to God that this were for Ireland!'

HANNA SHEEHY SKEFFINGTON

Suffragette and Feminist
1877–1946

JOHANNA MARY SHEEHY was born in May 1877 in Kanturk, County Cork, the daughter of David Sheehy, an Irish Parliamentary Party MP and former member of the Irish Republican Brotherhood, and niece of Fr Eugene Sheehy, known as the 'Land League priest'. The family moved to Dublin when Hanna was ten years old and she was sent to the Dominican Convent in Eccles Street. There her scholastic brilliance marked her out for an academic career, but because of the objections – often bitter – to third-level education for women, she had to graduate by the circuitous route of attendance at the Dominican-run St Mary's University College for Women and sitting the Royal University graduate examinations as an external student. She obtained a BA in modern languages in 1899 and an MA in the same subject in 1902. She joined the teaching staff of the Rathmines School of Commerce and was appointed examiner for the Intermediate Examination Board.

In 1903 she married the mildly eccentric Francis Skeffington, the university registrar of UCD, who took her name when she took his. One of her sisters, Mary, married Thomas Kettle, the writer and politician who was killed in action at Ginchy on the Somme in 1916, and another, Kathleen, was the mother of Conor Cruise O'Brien.

Francis resigned from his job after a dispute with the college president over the appointment of female academics. Already a pacifist (as well as vegetarian and teetotal), he joined in his wife's campaign for women's suffrage. Along with James and Margaret Cousins, they formed the militant Irish Women's Franchise League (IWFL) in 1908.

Already noted for her ability as a platform speaker who challenged the narrow norms of the Catholic Irish society of the day, Hanna caused a public scandal by refusing to have her son, Owen Lancelot, baptised. He would later carry on the family tradition of considered vocal criticism of self-satisfied Ireland.

In 1912 Hanna and her husband founded *The Irish Citizen*, a socialist paper meant to promote not just feminist ideals but the rights and responsibilities of all Irish citizens. She tended to be less pacifist than Francis, who, though active during the 1913 lockout, resigned from the Irish Citizen Army when it became militarised. In understandable pique at the lack of any mention of women's suffrage in Redmond's Home Rule

Bill, Hanna led a party of IWFL members to break windows in Dublin Castle in 1912 and, having made a fiery political speech in court, was sent to Mountjoy Prison for one month. She was imprisoned again for 'assaulting a policeman', a member of the Dublin Metropolitan Police, a force which required a minimum height of 6 feet, while she was just 5 feet 2 inches tall. She immediately went on hunger strike and was released after five days.

Both husband and wife were strongly against the recruitment drive when the Great War began in 1914, not fully aware of the almost hysterical elation in Britain. Francis was imprisoned for his protesting.

When the Volunteers rose in Easter Week 1916, because of his pacifist principles, Francis took no part except to try to dissuade looters. On the Tuesday evening he was arrested and taken to Portobello Barracks while handing out anti-looting leaflets. That evening Captain J. C. Bowen-Colthurst of the Royal Irish Rifles took Francis with him on patrol as a hostage, and Francis saw him deliberately shoot a boy called J. J. Coade. The next morning Francis and two journalists, Patrick McIntyre and Thomas Dickson, neither of whom had anything to do with the Rising, were shot on Bowen-Colthurst's orders, the bungled operation requiring two firing squads.

A grief-stricken but determined Hanna began a campaign to highlight this travesty of justice. A senior officer, Sir Francis Vane, insisted on a court martial for Bowen-Colthurst but, failing to get a response from the army, communicated directly with the secretary of state for war, Lord Kitchener, who ordered Bowen-Colthurst's arrest. The resulting court martial, held in June 1916, found Bowen-Colthurst of unsound mind. He was sent to Broadmoor Asylum but released on pension a year and a half later. Hanna fought on until a Royal Commission apologised for the killings and offered her compensation of £10,000 (about €350,000 today), which she refused. Francis' body, which had been buried in Portobello, was exhumed and re-interred in Glasnevin on 8 May 1916.

The following two years Hanna spent on a lecture tour in America, vigorously supporting Sinn Féin (she was a member of the executive) and the coming struggle for Ireland's independence. She spoke at 250 meetings, raising significant sums for Michael Collins, and published *British Militarism as I Have Known It*, which was banned in Britain until after the war. In January 1918 she presented the document stating Ireland's case for self-determination to the largely unheeding President Woodrow Wilson.

When Hanna attempted to return to Ireland, the British government refused her permission to enter the country. She managed to smuggle herself back, and was arrested and imprisoned under the Defence of the Realm Act in Holloway Prison in London. Also incarcerated there were Kathleen Clarke, the widow of the executed leader Tom Clarke, Constance Markievicz and Maud Gonne-MacBride. Hanna immediately went on hunger strike and was quickly released.

She was a staunch opponent of the 1921 Treaty with Britain and although she accepted a position on the executive of Fianna Fáil in 1926, she resigned in protest when de Valera took the oath to the king that enabled him and members of his party to enter the Dáil. She had also become aware that there was no place in an essentially conservative, male-dominated political party like Fianna Fáil for a committed radical and feminist.

Her campaign in 1935 against the Conditions of Employment Bill, which overtly discriminated against women, showed that she knew which way the political wind was blowing. Her worst fears were confirmed when the terms of the 1937 constitution were made known; there was no place in it for the feminist ideals for which she had fought all her adult life.

Hanna died on 20 April 1946 and is buried beside her husband in Glasnevin Cemetery.

JONATHAN SWIFT

Satirist
1667–1745

JONATHAN SWIFT was born on 30 November 1667 at 7 Hoey's Court, Dublin, at least seven months after his father, also Jonathan, died. His father was Irish and Hoey's Court, now gone, was then a good address close to Dublin Castle, between the cathedrals of Christ Church and St Patrick's. It is believed that his mother, Abigail Erick (or Herrick), returned to England as soon as she was fit to travel after his birth, leaving the infant in the care of his father's relatives. His uncle, Godwin Swift, acted *in loco parentis* and made sure that the boy received the finest possible education, sending him to Kilkenny Grammar School, then regarded as the best in the country. It was the Alma Mater of the dramatist William Congreve and the philosopher George Berkeley. In 1682 Swift entered Trinity College and graduated with a BA in 1686, after a far from distinguished academic career.

At the time Dublin was in turmoil, with a notable preference for Catholics while James II reigned. Swift, being a member of the Protestant Anglican High Church, went to England and was accepted into the house of Sir William Temple in Moor Park in Surrey as secretary. It was there he met eight-year-old Esther Johnson, nicknamed 'Stella', the housekeeper's daughter, with whom he was to have an ambiguous relationship for the rest of her life. It was also at Moor Park that Swift began to show signs of Ménière's disease, a disorder of the inner ear with distressing symptoms of giddiness, tinnitus and nausea that would plague him throughout his life, causing him often to fear for his sanity.

He returned to Ireland but was soon back in Moor Park, managing to obtain an MA from Hertford College, Oxford, in 1692 with help from Temple. Back in Ireland again, he was ordained in 1695 in the Church of Ireland and appointed to the parish of Kilroot, County Antrim, which had remarkably few Anglicans, set as it was in a strongly Presbyterian area. During his short-lived tenure there, he found himself strongly attracted to Jane Waring, an archdeacon's daughter, whom he renamed in his usual way with a Latinate nickname, 'Varina'. He asked her to marry him but when she demurred, drove her away with a bitterly cold letter written from Moor Park, where he stayed from 1696 until Temple's death in 1699.

Following this, Swift travelled back and forth to Ireland as a curate at Laracor, near Trim in County Meath, and prebendary of St Patrick's cathedral. He also graduated with a doctorate in divinity from Trinity in 1702 and was known thereafter as Dr Swift. His first brilliant works of satire, *A Tale of a Tub* and *The Battle of the Books*, savagely satirising the Church and literati of the time, were published anonymously in 1704, though as with all his work, everyone could recognise the mordantly witty style and the spare elegance of the prose.

His parish in Laracor had just fifteen churchgoers but he had a stipend that kept him financially afloat and he was free to travel frequently to London. It was probably the happiest time of his life, spending time with Alexander Pope, Joseph Addison and fellow Irishmen Richard Steele and John Gay, author of *The Beggar's*

Opera. The Bickerstaff Papers showed his brilliance as an essayist and from 1910 he wrote for the Tory party, lambasting their Whig opponents. However, in spite of much cultivation of politicians, the prize of archbishop of Dublin eluded him and he finally reluctantly accepted the deanery in St Patrick's cathedral in 1713. His exile in Dublin, as he saw it, became virtually permanent when the Whigs regained power in 1714.

While in Dublin his loathing of the human body and its animal functions grew almost to the point of neurosis. It is demonstrated in many of his poems, like 'A Beautiful Young Nymph Going to Bed' and 'The Lady's Dressing Room', and by his giving the debased Yahoos in *Gulliver's Travels* human shape. His poems run to 540 pages and have many tender and genuinely funny pieces, including 'Cadenus and Vanessa', a delicate account of his essentially platonic relationship with Esther Vanhomrigh – Cadenus an anagram of Decanus (dean) and Vanessa his pet name for her. It was ironic that *Gulliver's Travels*, written as a searing satire on contemporary British politics, should have essentially survived only in its first two parts and, even then, as a children's book.

Possibly his finest sustained piece of blistering satire, arising out of his hatred of the regime in Ireland, is *A Modest Proposal* (1729), in which with apparent reasonableness, he suggests that one solution to Ireland's economic crisis is the cannibalisation of the children of the poor. This pamphlet was the last of many attacks on the administration. Another of his works, *The Drapier's Letters,* led to the withdrawal of William Wood's right to mint copper coins in Ireland. Swift believed corruption had been involved in the granting of the patent to Wood. His writing gained him the reputation of being a patriot and let him claim that 'Fair Liberty was all his cry'. It also allowed him to include the words in his self-composed epitaph '… *imitare, si poteris/Strenuum pro virili/Libertatis vindicatorem*' ('match if you can this active champion of human freedom').

Apart from Varina, Vanessa and Anne Long (a London society beauty), the chief woman in Swift's life was Esther Johnson, his Stella. Their relationship was troubled, some suggesting that fear of a distant blood relationship prevented the morbidly sensitive Swift from consummation. However, rumours began after his death that they had been married in 1716, when Stella was thirty-five. His letters to her were undoubtedly loving and written in a special baby language they had devised between them during his days in Moor Park. Vanessa died of tuberculosis in 1723 and did not mention him in her will. Her death eased the tension that the rivalry between the two women caused Swift: Stella in Dublin and moving in society, Vanessa more isolated in

Celbridge, County Kildare. He was in England in 1727 when word came that Stella was dying. He hurried back to Ireland but could not bear to be there at the end.

Ménière's and dementia made his last years lonely and desolate. He died on 19 October 1745 and is buried by Stella's side in St Patrick's cathedral. The bulk of his fortune was left to found a mental hospital. As he wrote: 'He gave the little wealth he had/To build a house for fools and mad.' In his epitaph, he acknowledges the part played by *saeva indignatio* (cruel indignation) in his troubled life.

Swift was remembered by his depiction on the Irish £10 note.

THEOBALD WOLFE TONE

United Irishman
1763–1798

THEOBALD WOLFE TONE was born on
20 June 1763 at 44 Stafford Street (now
Wolfe Tone Street), Dublin, the son of Peter,
a prosperous coach builder who had land in
Bodenstown, County Kildare. His mother, Margaret Lamport, the daughter of a West Indies
trader, was Catholic but converted to Protestantism six years after his birth. Tone was a bright but
erratic student, capable of rapid study but more
interested in strutting about the city in gorgeous,
quasi-military garb. He decided to join the army
but his tolerant father for once put his foot down
and quick-marched him into Trinity College as
a 'pensioner' – the lowest level of fee-paying stu-

dent. His career at college was leisurely and he did not graduate until 1786, when he was twenty-three, but he had shown his capacity for scholarly labour when it was necessary by winning a scholarship in 1784.

While an undergraduate, he indulged in 'one or two fugitive passions' but two predominated: a two-year affair with Eliza Martin, the wife of 'Humanity Dick' Martin from Connemara, and a more decorous one with the fifteen-year-old Martha Witherington, with whom he eloped on 25 July 1785. His family's glacial reaction to this marriage took some time to mellow.

After a spell in the Middle Temple, Tone was called to the Irish bar in 1789. Martha was remarkable in her uncomplaining patience, even permitting her name to be changed to Matilda, the archetypical wife and mother from the play *Douglas*, in which Tone had appeared with Eliza, who played the character of that name. Tone had little relish for the practice of law but politics fascinated him. Though his voice was harsh and guttural, he was a compelling speaker and an even finer pamphleteer.

In September 1791, heady with the news of the revolution in France and conscious of the freedom of the newly declared United States of America – for white Anglo-Saxon Protestants at least – he published *An Argument on Behalf of the Catholics of Ireland*. It was written under the name 'Northern Whig', a *nom de guerre* he felt entitled to, since he had, at the request of Thomas Russell, formulated the resolutions for the celebrations of Bastille Day in Belfast. In it he named England as 'the never-failing source of all our political evils' and his ambition was 'to substitute the common name of Irishman in place of the denominations of Protestant, Catholic and Dissenter'.

In October, the Society of the United Irishmen was founded in Belfast, and Tone was actively involved in setting up this radical new movement.

Tone kept a journal for most of his adult life and in it he used nicknames for himself, his friends and even the town of Belfast. He was 'Mr Hutton', with the accent on the second syllable, Russell was 'PP' (clerk of this parish) and the town became Blefuscu after Lilliput's enemy in *Gulliver's Travels* written by his hero, Jonathan Swift.

In 1792 he was made the salaried (although sluggishly paid) secretary of the Catholic Committee that was to agitate for a Catholic Relief Act, which, when it came, was grievously disappointing.

Most of Tone's political and revolutionary activity was predicated upon help from France, a country that was suffering a long, drawn-out revolution and later Napoleonic autocracy. The generally one-sided love affair with France put Tone in danger of imprisonment more than once. The details of all the members and activities of the United Irishmen were being fed to the Dublin authorities by the master informer Leonard MacNally, who, ironically, was the advocate most used by them. When an incompetent spy for the French, Rev. William Jackson arrived, MacNally suggested that Tone should prepare a paper indicating the true state of feeling in the country. When this document was produced at Jackson's trial for treason-felony (during which he committed suicide in the dock by taking poison), Tone felt it advisable to leave the country.

He arranged to travel to Delaware with his wife and three surviving children, and since the port of embarkation was Belfast, there was an opportunity for a theatrical gesture of the kind that he loved. On 12 June 1795 he, Russell, Samuel Neilson and Henry Joy McCracken climbed to the highest point of Cave Hill, known as McArt's Fort, and vowed never to cease their struggle until they had 'subverted the authority of England'.

America proved to be a staging post and Tone found himself in France in February 1796. His eloquence was never used to better effect than in persuading the Directory (the committee which governed France) to assemble a fleet of forty-five ships and nearly 15,000 men under the command of Lazare Hoche, the leading French captain after Napoleon, to aid in an Irish rebellion. But when the grand fleet arrived in Ireland, it was forced to lie off Bantry Bay during Christmas 1796, unable to land its waiting soldiers because of a series of easterly storms, even though in

Tone's own words, 'We were near enough to toss a biscuit ashore.' With the fleet scattered and provisions running low, the ships that survived returned home without effecting their mission.

Disappointed but by no means daunted, Tone, now an adjutant general, was soon involved in another invasion scheme. On 8 July 1797 he boarded a ship of the Dutch fleet, hopefully named *Vrijheid* ('Freedom'). Again the winds turned against them and the armada was unable to sail. When it was finally able to set sail, Tone was not on board; he was in Wetzlar trying to persuade the terminally ill Hoche to take command. As he recorded in his journal for 23 December: 'It was well I was not on board the *Vryheid* [*sic*].' The Dutch fleet had been engaged by the English fleet at Camperdown and almost annihilated.

Tone made one last attempt to lead an invasion fleet, sailing from Brest around 20 September 1798 with 3,000 troops. They arrived at the entrance to Lough Swilly, on the north coast of Donegal, on 10 October, but before any troops could be landed, the French were engaged by a British fleet. Bompard, the French commander, advised Tone to leave in a fast-sailing schooner, but he refused and was captured. When he was brought ashore as a prisoner, one of the reception committee was Sir George Hill, MP for Derry and an old undergraduate acquaintance, who later remarked that Tone greeted him 'with as much sang-froid as you might expect from his character'.

Tone was taken to Derry Jail in leg-irons, still in the colourful uniform of a French colonel, and then to the Royal Barracks at Dublin Castle. On 10 November he was court-martialled and sentenced to be hanged in spite of his request 'to be shot by a platoon of grenadiers'. On the morning set for his execution, he cut his throat, injuring the windpipe but missing his jugular vein. He remarked to the émigré French surgeon who tended him, 'I find, then, that I am but a bad anatomist.' He lingered until 19 November, probably dying from septicaemia from the infected wound.

A statue of Tone surrounded by standing granite stones and sculpted by Edward Delaney stands at the north-eastern corner of St Stephen's Green; it is nicknamed 'Tonehenge'. Thomas Davis, whose hero Tone was, left a more lyrical memorial:

In Bodenstown churchyard there is a green grave,
And freely around it let winter winds rave –
Far better they suit him – the ruin and the gloom –
Till Ireland, a Nation, can build him a tomb.

AFTERWORD

This book is finished but it is far from complete. Small countries are often accused of exaggerated patriotism to compensate for perceived lack of stature. Yet it seems to me that Ireland can claim, without any boasting, a large number of heroes, however that word may be defined. There are an awful (in every sense of the word) lot of saints and scholars, for instance, who deserved inclusion: Columbanus, who, combining sanctity with scholarship, brought a kindly light to the Dark Ages; his disciple Gall, who is still revered in Switzerland; Fiachra, who gave his name to taxicabs during *la belle époque* Paris; and many many more, including St Patrick, who was really British. Scholars include John Scottus Eriugena, who wrote *De Divisione Naturae* and was promptly declared a heretic because his theory of life did not seem to tally with that of the Bible. Others who deserve similar memorials are Sedulius Scottus, who may have written 'Pangur Bán', and Diciul, the ninth-century geographer and astronomer.

If we go further back through the line between fact and fancy the place is leppin' with heroes. Was Brigid a saint or a repurposed Celtic goddess? Did Fionn Mac Cumhail once pacify the land for Cormac Mac Airt? Is Oisín really buried in the glens of Antrim? As the chequered history of Ireland unrolls, many others present themselves for inclusion with equal justice: Ruairí O'Connor, the last high king; Garrett Mór, the great Earl of Kildare; Aodh Ruadh, the wild prince of Tír Conaill; Dervorgilla, Princess of Breffni, who ran away with the king of Leinster, Dermot MacMurrough – the man who brought the Normans to Ireland; and Rosa O'Doherty, wife of Eoghan Rua.

The last two centuries, the ones we know most about, are literally full of remarkable and indomitable Irishry. It is only since then that women, no longer subject to gender disqualification, have been able to assert themselves. Mna na hÉireann have at last come into their own, and they and their courageous pioneers probably warrant another book of their own – but that could be objected to as discriminatory! As I was confined by space the only solution to this problem is perhaps another book of Irish heroes or maybe two!

The Irish, as a nation, have been accused of dwelling too much in the past. In fact, I feel, we do not dwell enough in it. I hope *Great Irish Heroes* will help correct that imbalance.

ALSO AVAILABLE FROM MERCIER PRESS

ISBN: 978 1 78118 413 5

The Illustrated Favourite Poems We Learned in School takes the most popular poems that Irish schoolchildren learned in school and pairs them with enchanting photographs, many of times past. With gems such as 'The Old Women of the Roads', 'Casabianca' and 'Sea-Fever', this is a collection to treasure.

www.mercierpress.ie